Anger, Aggression and Violence

Anger, Aggression and Violence

An Interdisciplinary Approach

by
PAUL R. ROBBINS

McFarland & Company, Inc., Publishers
Jefferson, North Carolina, and London

ISBN 0-7864-0903-7 (softcover : 50# alkaline paper) ∞

Library of Congress cataloguing data are available

British Library cataloguing data are available

Manufactured in the United States of America

*McFarland & Company, Inc., Publishers
Box 611, Jefferson, North Carolina 28640
www.mcfarlandpub.com*

To Arnold Meyersburg,
teacher and friend

Acknowledgments

The author would like to thank Dr. Sharon Hauge, Dr. Larry Robbins, George Lane and Martha Weaver for their contributions to the book. Grateful acknowledgment is made to the following for permission to reprint excerpts from their copyrighted materials: Alfred A. Knopf, a division of Random House, for B.W. Tuchman, *The First Salute*, E. Trinkaus and P. Shipman, *The Neandertals* and M. Friedman and D. Ulmer, *Treating Type A Behavior and Your Heart*; Jossey-Bass for J. Garbarino, *Raising Children in a Socially Toxic Environment*; Oxford University Press for F.E. Zimring and G. Hawkins, *Crime Is Not the Problem: Lethal Violence in America*; Harvard University Press for C. Jencks, *Rethinking Social Policy*; Allyn and Bacon for R.W. Novaco, "Clinical Problems of Anger and Its Assessment and Regulation Through Stress Coping Skills Approach," in W. O'Donohue and L. Krasner (eds.), *Handbook of Psychological Skills Training: Clinical Techniques and Applications*; The University of Nebraska Press for A.C. Huston, et al., *Big World, Small Screen: The Role of Television in American Society*; *Los Angeles Times* for "Understanding the Riots"; Houghton Mifflin for A. Hochschild, *King Leopold's Ghost* and R. Benedict, *The Chrysanthemum and the Sword*; Plenum Press for C. Wickless and I. Kirsch, "Cognitive Correlates of Anger, Anxiety and Sadness," *Cognitive Therapy and Research*, 12 (1988), 369–377; American Anthropological Association for E.L. Schieffelin, "Anger and Shame in the Tropical Forest: An Effect as a Cultural System in Papua New Guinea," *Ethos*, 11 (1983), 181–191; American Counseling Association for B.S. Sharkin, "Treatment of Client Anger in Counseling," *Journal of Counseling and Development*, 66 (1988), 361–365; American Orthopsychiatric Association for R.C. Herrenkohl, et al., "Preschool Antecedents of Adolescent Assaultive Behavior: A Longitudinal Study," *American Journal of Orthopsychiatry*, 67 (1997), 422–432; Heldref Publications for P.R. Robbins and R.H. Tanck, "Anger and Depressed Affect: Interindividual and Intraindividual Perspectives," *Journal of Psychology*, 131 (1997), 489–500; Elsevier Science for D.M. Buss and T.K. Shackelford, "Human Aggression in Evolutionary Psychological Perspective," *Clinical Psychology Review*, 17 (1997), 605–619.

Contents

Introduction

Hardly a day passes when a daily metropolitan newspaper does not report an incident of violence. It might be a story about a distraught man who killed his wife and then himself, or it might be an episode of terrorism in which a car bomb killed and wounded scores of people. Or it might be a brief story buried in the back pages about one of those seemingly intractable conflicts between ethnic groups in the Balkans, Africa or the Indian subcontinent.

For every story of violence that makes its way into the pages of the newspaper, there are many more that do not. They may be incidents of violence that find their way into police reports—or incidents that are never reported to anyone. Wife battering and child abuse are everyday occurrences that we as a society often overlook until they exceed our tolerance limits.

Violence has been a part of the human condition for a long time. Archeological research suggests that in early forms of hominids there are traces of violence inflicted by other hominids. Writing from the perspective of evolutionary psychology, David Buss and Todd Shackelford noted that "ancient hominid skeletal remains have been discovered that contain cranial and rib fractures that appear inexplicable except by the force of clubs and weapons that stab.... Fragments from the weapons are occasionally found lodged in skeletal rib cages."[1]

In their book *The Neandertals*, Erik Trinkaus and Pat Shipman describe the remains of a Neandertal male who was perhaps 30 to 45 years old when he died. The individual had been badly beaten by something, or more likely by somebody.

"Careful study of his bones revealed a plethora of serious but healed fractures. There had been a crushing blow to the left side of the head, fracturing the eye socket, displacing the left eye, and probably causing blindness on that side. He also sustained a massive blow to the right side of the body that so badly damaged the right arm that it became withered and useless ... the right foot and lower right leg were also damaged, possibly at the same time ... the right knee and various parts of the left leg also show signs of pathological damage; these may have been either further consequences of the same traumatic injury or lesions that developed in reaction to the abnormal limping gait that must have resulted from the damage to the right leg and foot."[2]

The violence inflicted on this Neandertal male sounds horrific. The history of our own species has more than its share of violent encounters—sometimes rising to the level of sheer brutality. We need not travel to foreign shores such as Bosnia or Rwanda to find appalling records of such brutality. America's own history has enough miserable moments. The poet Walt Whitman, an observer of the American Civil War who made numerous visits to the hospital bedsides of wounded soldiers, related the story of an attack of Confederate guerrillas under the command of John Mosby on an ambulance wagon train of wounded Union soldiers near Upperville, Virginia. About 60 wounded soldiers were in the wagons. The wagons were guarded by a small escort. When the guerrillas fell upon the outmanned escort, the Union forces surrendered. The guerrillas dragged the wounded soldiers from the wagons and began mutilating and killing them. Whitman described the case of one officer who was dragged on his back across the ground and surrounded by guerrillas. They thrust bayonets through his feet, pinning them to the ground. Then he was repeatedly stabbed in different parts of his body including his face and mouth. Whitman reports that the officer was stabbed 20 times. During the butchery a Union cavalry troop charged onto the scene, routing the guerrillas. Nineteen prisoners were taken. The officers were executed, then the men were told to run for their lives. A cordon of Union soldiers fired at the fleeing prisoners, killing every last man.[3]

In reading such reports, one might take a dim view of humanity, perhaps entertaining the thesis that violence is wired into our species. One can certainly argue that for our ancestors, the capacities to hunt game and to defend oneself against predators were survival skills. Granting this position, however, it does not mean that even wired-in violent tendencies cannot be diminished by appropriate socialization to the point that such tendencies may all but disappear. There are human societies in which violence is almost unheard of.

The assumption underlying this book is that in order to better understand violence, it is important to also examine anger and aggression, concepts that are related to violence but differ in significant ways. Feelings of anger often precede aggressive and violent acts. If we understand how to control anger better, we would expect a reduction in violence. And aggression, itself, may be channeled into behaviors that can be useful rather than destructive.

Our purpose will be to look at these three concepts and their interrelationships. The perspective of the author is that of a psychologist. But as the problem extends far beyond the borders of this discipline, we will draw on materials from anthropology, sociology and history as well as statistical data provided by criminologists.

The plan of the book is to first consider anger and aggression. Then we shall look at aggression and violent behavior in a cultural and historical context. Our focus will shift to how such behaviors are learned, drawing on research in developmental psychology. We will then discuss the implication that anger and aggression have for one's health and relationships. The succeeding chapters will consider factors (alcohol use and exposure to media violence) that may stimulate aggressive behavior and riots—the contagious violence that erupts in communities. The book will close with discussions of the treatment and prevention of violence.

CHAPTER 1

Anger

H e certainly looked calm enough when he sat back in his chair, smiled and told me, "I never get angry." I reflected for a moment and replied, "Do you mean by that—you never show your anger?" He nodded his head and then said, "Yeah—I never show it."

It's hard to imagine a person who *never* has experienced the feeling of anger. The emotion of anger is seemingly wired into our biology, although how we handle these feelings may vary widely from person to person. I remember a patient who exploded when he felt angry. His voice rose to near shouting levels. His facial expression transformed itself from its usually pleasant countenance to one that was seething with rage. His fists were clenched. He appeared livid. And his words matched his appearance. They were bitter, sarcastic and accusing.

Individual differences in the way we deal with anger are important because they influence both our own health and well being and the well being of others with whom we frequently interact. The quality and even the existence of our relationships can be affected by the way we deal with angry feelings.

Most of us recognize the vocalization of anger without difficulty. The tone of voice may be loud and strident, the words spoken convey irritation, disapproval. Even without vocalizations, the appearance of an angry face is something most of us are familiar with and can readily identify. To appreciate the mechanics of an angry expression, try following the instructions of mime performer and teacher David Alberts. While looking into a mirror, think of bringing all your facial muscles in toward the nose. Now, furrow your eyebrows and bring your mouth up in a tight-lipped frown.[1]

The philosopher Aristotle wrote more than 2000 years ago that "There are characteristic facial expressions which are observed to accompany anger, fear, erotic excitement, and all the other passions."[2] For anger and fear, at least, Aristotle's observations have proven essentially correct. Some classic studies carried out by Paul Ekman and by Carroll Izard have demonstrated that people can look through a series of photographs of faces and generally agree which of these facial expressions convey anger.[3] What Ekman and his colleagues did was to ask people to pose—in the manner of an actor—showing various emotions: happiness, surprise, disgust, sadness, fear, anger and contempt. From a pool of more than 3,000 photographs, they selected the pictures that best represented these emotions. Then they showed the pictures to people both here and abroad. The people were asked to match the facial photographs with the emotions listed above. Happiness was the easiest emotion to identify. Well over 90 percent of the research subjects correctly matched a smiling face with the descriptive term. The percentage of people correctly identifying anger was somewhat lower, running about 80 percent in Western societies. When the testing was done in non–Western societies (e.g., in Malaysia, Turkey, Ethiopia), the figures fell to about 60 percent, still far above what one might expect by chance.

The ability to identify anger from facial photographs may be universal in humans. Two researchers, J.D. Boucher and G.E. Carlson, ventured into the forests of Malaysia showing photographs posed by American men to 31 Temuans, a forest-dwelling people of Malay aborigines. When these people who had had only minimal contact with Western culture were asked to select an expression showing anger from the photographs, 73 percent chose the correct picture.[4]

Ekman believed that momentary facial expressions provide the key to recognition of emotions. He wrote, "The information they convey about an emotion can be captured in an instant. Typically, such expressions last a few seconds, but a single frame."[5] Registering an angry expression in another person is something like taking a snapshot. You see it and you know it. Ekman reported that while the expression of anger may vary from person to person with scores of shadings, there is a core configuration to these expressions that usually makes anger clear enough to those who witness it.

The Problem of Definition

While people are usually able to recognize anger when they witness it, anger has been surprisingly hard to define. This difficulty recalls the problems encountered in attempts to define pornography. A Supreme Court justice once remarked that while it was difficult to define pornography, he knew it when he saw it. Much the same thing can be said about anger. Anger is usually easy enough to recognize, but what exactly is it?

Some thoughtful psychologists have offered definitions of anger, but these definitions differ from one another. Here are a few examples:

> An internal state involving varying degrees and interactions between physiological, affective, cognitive, motoric, and verbal components [B.S. Sharkin, 1988].[6]

> I define anger as the elicitation of one or more aggression plans by the combination of threat appraisal and coping processes [Jeffrey Rubin, 1988].[7]

Some readers might be pausing at this point and shaking their heads. The terms used to define anger sound more complicated and obtuse than anger itself. Will the attempt to define anger only lead one on a semantic goose chase? The next definition, however, seems more comprehensible:

Anger can be understood as a subjective emotional state defined by the presence of physiological arousal and cognitions of antagonism (Raymond Novaco, 1994).[8]

We might also mention the views of Charles Spielberger and his colleagues, who described anger as an emotional state consisting of feelings that varied in intensity, from mild annoyance to intense rage.[9]

These definitions suggest that anger may be viewed as an emotional state that is linked on the one hand to certain types of thought processes and on the other to physiological reactions. This is a fair starting point, but hardly precise. Jeffrey Rubin noted that there was no generally agreed upon definition of anger. He wrote that "Some definitions are ambiguous about the presence or absence of relevant components, some define the components differently, and some explicitly include components that others explicitly exclude."[10]

Rubin called the situation a "mishmash."[11] If the definitions of anger are indeed a mishmash, we might ask, just how important is it that we have a precise definition of anger? After all, we all have a pretty good idea what it is. From a standpoint of carrying out scientific research, a clear definition of anger is useful. For example, researchers seeking to develop self-report (questionnaire) measures of anger find a definition of anger a useful guide when making up items. If the researcher's definition of anger includes antagonistic thoughts, the items chosen for the questionnaire would ask about such thoughts. The researcher might include items such as, "I have very negative opinions about certain people I know," or "Some people I know aren't worth a damn." If the researcher's definition of anger deals with bodily reactions, he or she might write items such as, "I often feel all steamed up," or "Some situations make my blood boil." Now these items use metaphors rather than precise psychological descriptions, but they would probably serve well if one's concept of anger includes physiological components.

An alternative view about definitions of emotions is that emotions like anger, anxiety and love are inherently diffuse and the attempt to tie them down to rigid verbal definitions may be somewhat quixotic. Working at the University of Winnipeg, James Russell and Beverley Fehr have been doing some interesting research on how people perceive the meaning of different emotions, including anger.[12] One technique they used was to show college students lists of words that seem to relate to anger (e.g., "hate," "rage," "irritation"). They asked the students to rate each word on a one-to-six scale as to how well the word fit into the category of anger. A rating of one would be an extremely poor example while a rating of six would be an extremely good example. Words such as "fury," "rage," "mad," "violent" and "hate" had high average ratings, 4.00 or above. Words such as "irritation" and "resentment" were in 3.00 to 4.00 range, while words such as "indignant" and "disgust" were in the 2.00 to 3.00 range. Fehr and Russell's studies indicate that the shared meaning of anger is limited. People will generally agree on best case examples (fury, rage, aggravation, hate and hostility), suggesting that there may be central or core meaning to the term. However, when one moves away from this core, the boundaries between what is anger and what is not become fuzzy. One person may think of "exasperation" as anger while another person may not. The same may be said of "revulsion," "grumpiness" and "disgust."

In his research on the identification of facial expressions, Ekman used the term "core configuration" to describe facial expressions of anger. It may be that anger has a generally recognizable central core but its boundaries are fuzzy. The context in which emotions occur may make a difference in whether the emotion can be defined as anger or something else.

The Psychological Context of Anger

In a 1983 paper published in the *American Psychologist,* James Averill demonstrated that we can learn a lot about the nature of anger by asking questions to people about the circumstances that give rise to anger.[13] Interestingly, he found that the targets of angry feelings were more often than not people who were well known and liked—even loved—by the person who was feeling angry. In most instances, angry feelings that arose were directed toward friends and intimates.

Averill's data suggest that what typically gives rise to anger is a perceived misdeed. Averill observed that this was "perhaps the most important fact about anger."[14] The person who has become angry believes that he or she is responding to a provocation—a statement or act by another person that was both voluntary (unprovoked) and unjustified. In contrast, the person whose actions triggered the anger may feel that his or her behavior was justifiable: "I had a right to do what I did or say what I said," or it was unavoidable, "It couldn't be helped."

Some writers have used the term transgressions rather than misdeeds.[15] In studying the situations that people remembered in the marital relationship that triggered angry feelings, Julie Fitness and Garth Fletcher emphasized the perceived unfairness in these acts: "Unlike love, hate, or jealousy, anger tended to be elicited by the perception of having been treated unfairly by the partner."[16] One of their research subjects was angry "because his wife would not change her schedule so that he could have the car one evening. A major factor in his anger was his perception that he always 'went out of his way' to help her and consequently deserved better treatment. Other examples included subjects being blamed for accidents, being expected to do more than their 'fair share' of chores, and not having an equal say in decision making."[17] When the partner's perceived misdeed reached the level of bad treatment or humiliation, the response reached the level of hatred.

Averill's data suggest that provocations are typically interpersonal. One can get angry at a car for not starting, but one is more likely to become angry with a friend, coworker or spouse for an alleged misdeed. Roland Tanck and I collected data from college students concerning their angry feelings that confirmed that interpersonal difficulties were the most frequent sources of anger. We asked the students to fill out questionnaire-like diaries each night before they went to bed for a period of ten days.[18] One of the questions in the diary asked whether the student felt angry or annoyed that day. This was followed by a probe asking what it was that made the student feel angry. Looking through these data, we were able to sort most of the responses to the probe into four categories: (1) the source of anger was perceived as interpersonal (e.g., arguments, confrontations); (2) the source of the anger was perceived as academic (e.g., homework, tests); (3) the source of the anger was perceived as environmental or circumstantial (e.g., the weather, traffic jams, crowded dormitory); and (4) the source of anger was perceived as the self (self-criticism and self-reproach).[19]

The task of classifying the students' responses into these categories could be performed objectively. Two people working independently made these characterizations with very high agreement.

We found that the most frequent attribution for the cause of angry feelings was interpersonal difficulties. In a sample of 77 students, 74 reported feeling angry during the ten-day period and of these, only three did not on at least one occasion attribute their aroused anger to the actions of another person.[20]

In their responses, there were many illustrations of what Averill would have called "perceived misdeeds." Here are a few examples[21]:

"Someone broke the doorknob on my door."

"Our unreasonable landlord."

"My boyfriend flirting with everyone under the sun at a party."

"The constant, unrelenting kidding I had to take from my friends."

"My roommate, through his carelessness, clogged the kitchen sink."

"My roommate gave something I needed to someone and did not bring it back."

"The girl who stayed at our apartment till late afternoon and my sister and I both told her we had a lot of studying to do."

"My roommate was watching TV so loud you could hear it down the hall."

"A friend made some cutting remarks."

Perceived misdeeds or transgressions often center on the routine activities of living and work and the source of the misdeed is often a friend or intimate. Perceived misdeeds may be both acts of commission and acts of omission. Think about an instance where you depended on a person to do something and he or she didn't come through. You may have reacted with both anger and disappointment. Like deliberate provocative acts, acts of omission can have deleterious effects on the strength and vitality of relationships.

As one must expect, the students frequently attributed their angry feelings to academic pressures and constraints. Situational and environmental factors were atypical reasons. Least often, the students looked inwardly for reasons for feeling angry. Only 17 of the 74 students who reported feeling angry did this at all during the ten-day period and self-attribution usually happened only once.[22] Perceived misdeeds by oneself included some sins of commission ("An argument with a friend caused by a stupid thing I did") but were more likely to be sins of omission ("I got mad at myself for not doing better on the test," "My indecision and frustration," "My inability to study," "My loss of confidence within myself").[23] We shall see later that this confluence of anger and disappointment with oneself often plays a part in bringing on depressed feelings.

Both Averill's data and our own suggest people often attribute their angry feelings to the perceived misdeeds of another individual or individuals. What happens when the source of angry feeling is perceived as academic, as was often the case in our student sample? In their complaints about college life, students are sometimes able to point to a given individual—such as a teacher—as the source of the problem. Cynthia Wickless and Irving Kirsch describe an incident in which a student became very angry when a book she purchased for a course proved to be of no help on the exam. "I spent $26 for this book and a lot of time reading it.... I took the exam and there was not *one* question from the book.... I was led to believe—over and over—that this book was crucial.... I was misled and I spent time and money needlessly ... and both the money and the time are important to me."[24]

Often the perceived misdeed in academia cannot be attributed to any clear-cut source. The system itself may be viewed as being at fault. Many students perceive college life as making too many demands on them with too little time to meet these demands. While the system may be viewed as unfair, responsibility for setting up the system is unclear and diffuse. It may not be possible to blame a specific individual for one's problems. The student's response is one of frustration, anxiety and vaguely targeted anger. The same feelings may be engendered when one is employed in a large organization, particularly one that is bureaucratic.

When the cause of one's angry feelings is attributed to circumstances or the environment, it may be even more difficult to point to some willful act. Who is to blame for the car not starting or the inclement weather? A textbook exception to this truism was related by the Greek historian Herodotus. Xerxes, ruler of the ancient Persian empire, had made preparations to invade Greece with a large army. The invasion route included a bridge that his engineers had constructed over the Hellespont, the narrow waterway that separates Greece from Asia Minor. Now it happened that a great storm arose and destroyed the bridge. In his wrath, Xerxes ordered that the Hellespont should receive 300 lashes. The persons delivering the blows were said to have called out, "Thou bitter water, thy lord lays on thee this punishment because thou hast wronged him without a cause."[25] Xerxes must have perceived some misdeeds among the bridge builders as well, for while the river was being punished, the overseers of the work were beheaded.

Anger is a frequently felt emotion. Citing research reports scattered over a 60-year period (1918–1979), Averill observed, "Depending on how records are kept, most people report becoming mildly to moderately angry anywhere from several times a day to several times a week."[26] Our studies using the student diaries indicated that anger was reported on nearly 40 percent of the days sampled.[27]

Measuring Anger

Sometimes anger appears as a transient emotion; feelings are aroused and then dissipate. Sometimes anger seems to be more of a chronic condition. You might speak of someone you know as "an angry person." There is a parallel here with anxiety and depression. Some people may feel anxious at times while others seem chronically anxious. The same is true for people with depressed feelings.

In devising measures of anger, researchers have tried to differentiate transient anger from chronic anger. One approach researchers have used to measure transient angry feelings is a technique called the Adjective Check List. The Adjective Check List is a rather simple device that often yields useful results. Imagine a list of words arranged alphabetically perhaps starting with words like "affectionate," "blue," "cautious," "energetic" and "fearful." Imagine further that you are asked whether the word describes how you feel at the moment—using such benchmarks as "not at all," "a little bit" and "definitely." To sample angry feelings, you will see included in the list words such as "angry," "defiant" and "rebellious." Vincent Nowlis and Helen Green devised such an adjective check list in the 1950s. It yields a rough, instant snapshot of a transient angry mood.[28]

In the 1980s, Charles Spielberger used a more traditional test-making approach to develop standardized measures of transient anger, which he called "state" anger, and chronic anger, which he called "trait" anger. The scale measuring state anger consists of ten items that convey core feelings of anger such as feeling "furious." The person is asked to respond to each item on a four-point scale that ranges from not at all describing the person's present feelings to very much describing them. If state anger is measured at one point in time with this scale and rechecked two weeks later, there is unlikely to be much relationship because one is measuring a transitory phenomenon.[29]

Trait anger is conceived as a more lasting characteristic. Spielberger's measure of trait anger uses items that talk about a person being hot headed or quick tempered. The trait scale, too, consists of ten items and uses a four-point scale but unlike the state scale, scores over a two-week period tend to be reasonably stable.[30]

A third approach to developing self-report measures of anger is to present subjects with brief descriptions of situations that might be expected to provoke anger, such as "someone calls you a liar." The test-taker is asked to gauge the degree to which he or she would become angry in such a situation. Perhaps the most widely used of this type of anger measure was devised by Raymond Novaco.[31] The scale consists of 80 brief descriptions. For each item the subjects respond on a five-point scale to indicate how much anger would be aroused. Anger scores tend to be stable when subjects are retested over a period of one month, suggesting that the scale assesses trait anger rather than transitory feelings.

When researchers analyzed the content of the items in Novaco's scale, they found that the items tended to cluster into three types: injustice/unfairness, frustration/clumsiness and physical affronts.[32] Injustice and unfairness and physical affronts sound very much like the concept of perceived misdeeds.

Anger and Other Emotions

My clinical experience has been that anger often arises in the context of tension or stress. Some people become irritable and easily angered when they feel tense. Roland Tanck and I carried out some studies on the way people cope with stress that support this view.[33] We asked university students what things they did when they were feeling tense or anxious to diminish or relieve these uncomfortable feelings. We provided the students a checklist of items, which eventually grew to 42 items. The students were asked to respond to each item on a four-point scale ranging from "never" to "almost always." While not strictly a coping technique, we included an item "become irritable and easily angered." The item was frequently checked. For our male subjects, the mean value on the four-point scale of usage placed it in the upper quartile of behaviors listed (ranked ten out of 42). The mean score for usage exceeded those for "daydreams or fantasize," "get some vigorous exercise," or "talk to members of your family."

The students' responses indicated that having one's threshold become lower for feeling irritable and angry when tense was a common experience, but they did not see it as a particularly useful thing to happen. When asked about their view of the effectiveness of the different items ("put an '*' before any of the items which you have found in your own experience to be helpful"), the item ranked very low on the list. Interestingly, people who reported that they often become irritable and easily angered when tense had higher scores on a widely used instrument measuring depression—the Beck Depression Inventory. These data suggest that while anger may occur as an isolated phenomenon, it often occurs in the context of other emotions. In our studies using the student diaries, Tanck and I provided additional data that showed how feelings of anger may fall within a larger cluster of emotions. The diary contains many questions asking about a person's experiences and feelings during the day, and with the aid of a statistical technique called factor analysis, we were able to determine which of the responses to these questions tended to cluster together. Factor analysis revealed that our question asking whether the students had felt angry or annoyed during the day was part of a larger factor. Other diary items in the factor asked the students whether they had during the day expressed feelings of anger or annoyance, felt trapped in an uncomfortable situation, had to defend themselves, experienced defeat or frustration, felt rebuffed or hurt, felt tense or anxious or were given a hard time by someone.[34]

Two of the items—being given a hard time and feeling rebuffed or hurt by someone—recall Averill's concept of perceived misdeeds. The components of this factor—being provoked, hurt, and trapped, feeling frustrated and tense, having to defend oneself, and feeling and expressing anger—suggest a stressful, confrontational situation. We named the factor "interpersonal stress." Interpersonal stress is not the only pattern in which anger is an important component, but is certainly one that is commonly encountered in everyday life.

Denise, a woman in her mid–20s, is a good example of a person experiencing these feelings. Denise is bright and college educated. She had recently moved into the city and felt lonely. One night she met Don at a bar. He was a good-looking, but not well educated, man who did construction work for a living. They had an affair and Denise became pregnant. Shortly after the pregnancy was discovered, they married and moved into a small apartment. When their daughter Jill was born, Denise stayed home to take care of the baby during the daytime and at night she took a job waiting on tables in a restaurant to earn money to help pay the bills. It was a hard job: her boss was explosive and demanding. When she came home, she already had experienced all the criticism she could take. She had listened to too many complaints about what she hadn't done right. And now, at home, she often found Don tired and irritable after a long day of work and the baby fussing and needing attention. When Don began to complain about the way the apartment looked, the criticism stung her. She felt she was doing as much as she could and her efforts were unappreciated. The anger within her swelled and at times she exploded.

Hostility

In our discussion of anger so far, we have rarely used the word "hostility." There is much overlap between the words anger and hostility; sometimes the words are used interchangeably. What distinguishes hostility from anger is the attitudes that are characteristic of hostility. Hostility carries with it feelings of dislike often accompanied by negative evaluations. People who are hostile toward others may not only dislike a person or group of persons, they may disparage their behavior, values and character. They may distrust the person or persons and be suspicious of their intentions towards themselves and people like themselves.

The basis of this dislike might be unpleasant experiences with the person or persons or it could be statements one heard from others. To some extent, we are all influenced by the views of our elders as we grow up and by the peers that surround us. Historically, the attitudes that have been communicated in mainstream American society about groups not in the mainstream (e.g., immigrants, poor people, people of African descent, religious minorities) have contained negative, sometimes stereotyped evaluations. Sometimes these perceptions can be so negative that individuals or groups are demonized. Labels are tools in this process. During the First World War, Germans were referred to as "Huns." Hostility can fuel aggressive acts, even horrific acts of violence. In the 1990s in Bosnia, ethnic hostilities erupted into violence and gave rise to atrocities.

These initial explorations leave us with some tentative observations about anger. We will think of anger as an emotional state usually triggered by perceived misdeeds, perceptions of unfairness, and by the frustrations encountered in daily life. Angry feelings vary in intensity from borderline states such as annoyance and irritation to an almost unmistakable core state of rage. Anger may be transitory or it may occur often enough to be a chronic condition. As we shall see in later chapters, chronic anger has significant implications for one's health and well-being.

CHAPTER 2

Aggression

L ike anger, aggression has a core appearance that is almost unmistakable. Consider a schoolyard bully who approaches another child engaged in peaceful, solitary play and starts beating him up. This is an act of blatant aggression. No doubt about it. But like anger, the definition of aggression can become fuzzy when we move away from such unprovoked physical assaults to other behaviors. How about a wife who is angry and won't talk to her husband for a day? Is that prolonged silence aggression? Many psychologists would say "yes."

Aggression is not usually thought of as an emotional state like anger but as an act. In essence, an aggressive act is intended to inflict harm of some kind. Targets may be wide-ranging; other persons, oneself in the case of suicidal attempts, animals in the case of hunters, those pesky insects flying around one's summer barbeque or more rarely like Xerxes' lashing of the Hellespont, a non-living object. When the target is another human being, the harm intended is usually physical or psychological, though it can be social or economic as well.

In considering the relation of anger and aggression, it is tempting to set up a simple formula: anger is the emotion, the motivating, generating force that gives rise to aggression, the act. You feel angry; you strike the person or more likely say something hurtful. While this simple formula often works in explaining many aggressive acts, it is far from a perfect model. For one thing, angry feelings are not always followed by aggressive acts. In the data Tanck and I collected, we looked at a sample of 280 days in which students reported feeling angry. When we asked a follow-up question, "Did you express anger to anyone today?" in 70 percent of the instances, the students replied, "yes." So on many of the days (30 percent), angry feelings were not followed by clear-cut aggressive acts.[1]

Averill reported data that is consistent with ours. He found that when people said they had been angry, the usual "impulse" was to react aggressively (in about 82 percent of the episodes). However, their actual response was about as often nonaggressive as aggressive. "The most frequent responses were ... engaging in calming activities (in 60 percent of the episodes) and talking the incident over with the instigator (in 59 percent of the episodes). Aggression, when it did occur, was primarily verbal or symbolic (in 49 percent of the episodes)."[2] Physical aggression other than punishing children was infrequent. Clearly, aggressive impulses are often restrained and inhibited.

Among adults, aggressive acts typically occur with the failure of other actions that attempt to deal with perceived provocations in a more conciliatory manner. Joseph Mikolic and his colleagues identified a sequence of escalating responses to provocation beginning with a simple request for change.[3] Imagine someone is playing a television set at a very high volume in the next room. An initial civil response might be something like, "Please turn the T.V. sound down." When requests fail, demands follow, such as "Turn the sound down!" When demands fail, complaints begin. "You have the T.V. set much too loud. I can't concentrate." When complaints fail, angry remarks are next in line, followed by threats, harassment and abuse. For most people violence is the last resort. However, for some people, it may be the first action taken. Consider these two incidents.

Incident one was related to me by a college professor. She was driving her car to the campus when suddenly she struck a young man riding a bicycle. As she left the car to offer assistance, the young man rose to his feet. He smiled, put his arm around her shoulder and said, "Thank God, nobody is hurt." Relieved, the woman asked whether there were any damages to his bicycle that she could pay for. He checked the bicycle and replied that everything was fine, then he rode away.

Incident two was reported in a newspaper. A young man riding a bicycle was bumped by a car driven by a woman. The man fell off the bicycle. As the woman stopped the car and pulled over, the man rose to his feet and approached the car. He cursed the woman, pulled out a handgun and shot her in the head. A few minutes later she died. The man, apparently unhurt by the accident, fled on foot. He was arrested and charged with murder.[4]

We have seen that aggression may or may not occur when a person feels angry, that anger is often restrained. Looking at the other side of the coin, some aggressive acts may occur without clear-cut feelings of anger. Consider a mother disciplining a disobedient child. The mother has always believed in the dictum "Spare the rod and spoil the child." She had no intention of spoiling her child and when he misbehaved in the supermarket, knocking some boxes off the shelf, she spanked him immediately. If you asked her, she would assert that she wasn't really angry, that disciplining him was part of the job of being a mother. "He had to learn," she might say. In fact, she might accompany the spanking with an expression such as, "This hurts me more than it hurts you."

Certainly some parents who strike their children feel angry, if not furious. Child abuse is all too frequent in the United States. But not every act of punitive discipline is based on anger. The woman's act was based on a widely held theory of child raising that she learned from her parents.

The classic case of aggression that may take place with minimal anger is athletic competition. If you ever played football, basketball or some other contact sport, you may have been knocked around a bit. Blocking and tackling are aggressive acts, bodies colliding with considerable force. Yet the opponents who competed on the field may share a soft drink or beer afterwards in a spirit of camaraderie. It's usually only when someone breaks the rules under which these aggressive acts take place that tempers flare, such as incidents of "high sticking" in a hockey game, elbows thrown under the backboard in a basketball game or "unnecessary roughness" in a football game.

Writing in *Psychology Today*, Edwin Kiester noted that in organized sports, some coaches have tried to get their players mad at their opponents.[5] The theory is that such anger will get the player's adrenaline pumping, enabling them to perform at higher levels. However, Kiester also noted that high levels of anger can destroy concentration, and that some of the best athletes, even when provoked, keep their anger under control.

There are certainly examples of athletes who become angry and mean on the field. In professional baseball, the legendary Ty Cobb had a terrible reputation for using the spikes on his shoes against other players when sliding into bases. One time Chicago Bear linebacker Ron Rivera said he became a madman when he got on the field. He became mean, nasty and rotten, with no regard for the human body.[6] Still, even in organized sports, anger may be a minimal, even nonexistent precursor to physical aggression.

In his book *Civil Wars*, John Feinstein describes the highly competitive tradition of the Army-Navy football games. On the field the members of the teams gave everything they had to win—and that meant pushing, shoving, banging and tackling. But one does not sense high levels of anger. Feinstein tells the moving story of a member of the Army team who, after an Army victory, was so concerned about the disappointment he knew the Navy Team would experience, he went over to the Navy Team's locker room to console a player he had met on the team.[7]

When a hunter shoots a deer standing in the woods and kills it, was the motivation for this fatally aggressive act anger or was it something else? The American writer John Steinbeck thought that the act was related to masculinity. Steinbeck disparaged the skill of some hunters, relating a story of how a farmer hung a sign on both sides of his white cow during hunting season, stating in bold black letters that the animal was a cow. The cow was still killed by a hunter.[8] When American sailors fired Cruise missiles at Baghdad during the Gulf War, were they firing out of anger or did they see it as a job to do?

So, we must keep in mind that while anger does not always lead to aggression, aggression does not always presuppose anger.

Instrumental vs. Reactive Aggression

All aggressive acts have in common the core feature of trying to inflict harm or injury in some form on others. However, it is often possible to make a distinction between aggressive acts that are deliberately planned for the purpose of achieving some material gain (e.g., robbing a convenience store) and aggressive acts that are reactive (e.g., striking someone when provoked). We might add a third case when aggressive acts occur without any clear-cut reason or provocation; perhaps the offender has nourished grievances from perceived past injustices that are displaced onto targets of opportunity. Such acts may seem utterly senseless. When an aggressive act is clearly designed to achieve some material gain, psychologists have called such acts "instrumental aggression."[9]

While the distinction between instrumental and reactive aggression is a useful one, it is clear that many people are capable of both. A mugger who robs a woman of her purse then beats her senseless steals for gain and inflicts pain over and beyond the theft. In a study of incarcerated violent criminals, Dewey Cornell and his colleagues found that reactive offenders were more likely than instrumental offenders to know their victims, to be angry with them, and to act violently in a state of anger.[10]

Instrumental and reactive violent offenders were compared on a psychological screening instrument measuring psychopathic tendencies (being irresponsible, manipulative, lacking remorse, etc.). Instrumental offenders tended to have higher scores on this instrument than reactive offenders; they appear more cold-blooded about what they are planning to do.

The Measurement of Aggression

Researchers have attempted to measure aggressive behavior in several ways. These methods include direct observation, self-report measures and experimental procedures. Direct observation is an intuitive way of assessing aggressive behavior, for aggressive acts are visible to the eye and aggressive words can be heard or recorded. The method has been particularly useful in studying aggression in young children whose rates of aggressive responding are often high. Moreover, children can be studied in circumscribed environments such as day care centers and school playgrounds. In early studies the observer used a notebook and pen. Now technology permits researchers to use video cameras and, if desired, to place wireless microphones on the children.

A common procedure is to observe and record time samples of behavior. The researcher watches a particular child for a given period of time, say ten minutes, and dutifully notes what happens. If in the eleventh minute, the observed child clobbers another child, tough luck. The way around this problem is to supplement time-sampling with a "critical incident" technique, recording behaviors of interest whenever they occur. This will help the researcher judge the meaningfulness of the time-sampled data.

Here is an example of a recent study that used observation as the primary method of data-gathering.[11] The boys and girls who participated in the study were elementary school children. Some of the students who participated had been selected by their teachers as aggressive children, while others were selected as non-aggressive children. The two groups of children were matched on age, gender and ethnicity. Cameras positioned in classrooms overlooking the playground were used to obtain the observational data. When a child was being filmed, he or she wore a wireless microphone to record conversations. The plan was to observe each child during unstructured play time for four ten-minute time periods. Analysts coded the videotapes for various behaviors including verbal attacks and physical aggression. The researchers, Debra Pepler and her colleagues, reported that on average, the teacher-selected aggressive children engaged in physical aggression (hitting, kicking, punching) once every 6.6 minutes. The comparable figure for the teacher-chosen nonaggressive children was once every 11 minutes. Verbal attacks took place on average once every 17 minutes for the aggressive children as against once every 49 minutes for the nonaggressive children.

As was the case for anger, it is possible to obtain self-report measures of a person's propensity to become aggressive. Working initially with A. Durkee and later with Arnold Perry, Arnold Buss developed a questionnaire-like measure of hostility and aggression.[12] The latest incarnation of the scale is called the Aggression Questionnaire. Included are groups of items that deal with physical aggression (e.g., getting into fights, hitting back when attacked and breaking things) and verbal aggression (e.g., disagreeing with people, being argumentative and telling people what one thinks of them).

Scores for both measures, physical and verbal aggression, proved to be reasonably stable when people were tested at intervals of nine weeks, suggesting that the tendency to act aggressively may be viewed as a personality characteristic or trait. To check the validity of these self-report measures, the researchers compared the scores obtained from their Aggression Questionnaire with the assessments of people who knew those who filled out the questionnaire. The subjects in this validity study were members of college fraternities. Each fraternity member filled out the questionnaire and was also asked to list the names of his fraternity brothers who met the following descriptions:

1. Who is physically aggressive? Who hits if provoked? Who pushes or hits others even in play? Who fights physically to defend his beliefs?

2. Who is verbally aggressive? Who argues a lot? Who likes to debate every issue? Who uses strong language to cut people down? Who yells in arguments?

The researchers reported that the Aggression Questionnaire was more successful in identifying the fraternity members who were judged by their peers to be physically aggressive than those who were verbally aggressive.

Psychologists have devised experimental procedures that yield measures of individual differences in aggressive responding. In one type of procedure, the subject, usually a college student, is told that he or she is participating in a teacher-learner task.[13] The subject and a confederate of the experimenter are told that the subject will play the role of the teacher, the confederate that of the learner. The subject is instructed to administer electric shocks to the confederate when he or she makes an error on the task. The subject is asked to set the level of shock that will be administered. While no shocks are actually delivered, the subjects do not know this, and the level that he or she sets on the dial is a measure of aggressive responding.

It is also possible to study the psychological and physical aspects of aggressive behavior using games and simulations. Researchers have studied the reactions of people playing violent video games. Virtual reality games provide even more direct assessment of how people react under the appearance of physical threat. Sandra Calvert and Siu-Lan Tan placed their subjects—college students—into a virtual reality game in which one sees an armed opponent on a platform connected to other platforms by stairs.[14] The edges of the platforms end in dark space. Overhead, a prehistoric pterodactyl flies about attempting to pick up each player, lift them into the sky and drop them. As a player in this bizarre world, you have a device that enables you to take evasive action, moving from platform to platform. You also have a weapon that can shoot both your opponent and the pterodactyl. A hit is followed by an explosion. The game lasts four minutes.

Compared to people who merely observed the game, the players reported feeling dizzy and nauseated. Their pulse rates rose about 10 beats per minute. They were more likely to experience aggressive thoughts during the game than people who observed the game. The reactions of the women who played the game were not that distinguishable from those of the men. The researchers concluded that in this simulated combat situation, violent interactions overrode other characteristics such as gender and even peaceful personality predispositions resulting in similar aggressive effects for all participants.

Aversive Environments and Aggression

In an essay on aggression, Leonard Berkowitz pointed out that unpleasant events of many kinds, "whether they produce physical pain or discomfort or psychological distress," evoke "instigation to escape *and* to attack."[15] Fight and flight options both surface.

Berkowitz went beyond aggressive acts provoked by the misdeeds or attacks of another person and talked about the effects of an aversive environment. Aversive environments foster an instigation to aggression. He cited studies in which two animals (laboratory rats) were cooped up in a small chamber and subjected to aversive conditions such as electric shocks or loud noises. The animals often reacted by fighting. If given the option the animals might have simply escaped from the situation. However, when confined, they often turned on each other. The speculation is that these reactions may be defensive in part, perhaps instinctional.

Berkowitz noted that a variety of aversive conditions in human environments may increase the instigation to aggression. In experimental studies, foul odors, irritating cigarette smoke and high room temperatures increased the tendency of people to show hostility or mete out punishment to others. The relation of temperature and violence is an issue that has intrigued people for many years. In *Romeo and Juliet*, Shakespeare wrote, "I pray thee, good Mercutio, let's retire; the day is hot, the Capulets abroad and, if we meet, we shall not 'scape a brawl, for now, these hot days, is the mad blood stirring."[16]

Shakespeare was right on the mark. A host of studies have shown that higher temperatures are associated with higher rates of aggressive acts. For example, researchers found that homicide rates were higher in the Southern states of the United States than in the Northern states. One might argue that this might reflect a cultural difference as much as a temperature difference. Do you remember the scene in the classic film *Gone with the Wind* in which a hot-blooded Southern youth comes close to challenging crack shot Rhett Butler (played by Clark Gable) to a duel because Butler doubted the ability of the South to prevail in a war with the North? The temperature explanation looks the more likely, however, for similar trends were uncovered in Europe. Researchers reported that homicide rates increased as one drove from northern Italy to southern Italy. Homicide rates were much higher in the south of England than in the north. Assault rates were twice as high in southern France as they were in the rest of the country.[17]

If you consider violent crime you will find that rates peak in the summer and, excluding the Christmas season, are lowest in the winter. Again, one could suggest alternative explanations. More people are milling about on the streets in the summer months. Still, if one looks within the warmest months of the year one finds an effect. In a study carried out in Des Moines, Iowa, during July and August, it was found that there was more violent crime on hotter days than cooler days. And what is particularly important, this tendency was not found for non-violent crime.

Finally, researchers looked at a span of more than 40 years (1950 to 1995), computing the average temperature for each year. When they examined the murder and assault rate for each year, they found that the combined murder and assault rate was consistently higher in the hotter years than in the cooler years.

Reviewing the wide array of studies relating temperature and aggression, Craig Anderson concluded, "Clearly, hot temperatures produce increases in aggressive motives and tendencies. Hotter regions of the world yield more aggression; this is especially apparent when analyses are done within countries. Hotter years, quarters of years, seasons, months, and days all yield relatively more aggressive behaviors such as murders, rapes, assaults, riots, and wife beatings...."[18]

Frustration and Aggression

In certain areas of Washington, D.C., it is very difficult to find a parking space. On one city block, drivers simply cruise around the block hoping against hope that someone will pull out, vacating a parking space. One day, two people in a car were circling the block in this frustrating quest when suddenly a parking space opened up some distance behind them. A woman quickly alighted from the car and dashed into the space to hold it. She stood there warding off other drivers while her companion continued driving around the block. While the woman waited, a driver in another car stopped and was not deterred by her presence. The driver backed right toward the woman, who would not budge. She alleged that the driver ran over her foot. In an act of instant retaliation, she smashed the window of his car.[19]

In 1939 a group of psychologists at Yale University wrote a short monograph proposing that aggression was caused by frustration.[20] It was a relatively simple idea that was very influential. When the Yale psychologists were talking about frustration, they were talking about being thwarted in the pursuit of a goal, much like the aforementioned drivers in their search for a parking space. A prototype example would be a child who wants some attractive candy she sees in the supermarket. Her mother says "no." The child is motivated, the goal is visible, and she is denied. The theory proposed by the Yale group would hold that the child's propensity to react aggressively is increased. The aggressive act, however, may be inhibited, if the child has a fear that the act may elicit punishment. Still, some children may take the risk and make enough of a fuss that the mother will yield. In this case, the aggressiveness paid off, reinforcing a tendency for the child to become aggressive when frustrated.

The Yale group's formulation suggested that the likelihood of aggression occurring in response to frustration would increase when the goal in mind was perceived as important. Taking another example from children, if a boy had his heart set on playing football and his father said "no," telling him that he had to clean up his room, the chances of the boy's becoming unruly would be a lot higher than if he were told he couldn't do something he had only a mild interest in, such as watching a television program.

The Yale group also suggested that repeated frustrations are more likely to evoke an aggressive reaction than a single event. Consider a driver returning home from the office during rush hour traffic. After an hour of minor impediments slowing down his progress (waiting at traffic lights, avoiding construction zones, following an excessively slow driver), he may cross a threshold where he may explode at the next perceived bottleneck.

It wasn't long after the publication of the frustration-aggression formulation that critics raised objections to the theory. It was argued that whether a person became aggressive would depend on the way the frustration was perceived. An example offered was of a bus that didn't stop to pick you up while you were waiting at the stop. If it were pouring down rain and there were empty seats in the bus, you might utter a string of expletives. On the other hand, if the bus were jammed full of people, you might consider the act of not stopping reasonable. You would be no less wet but probably less miffed.

The perception of fairness and feelings of relative deprivation certainly influence reactions to frustration. If in a frustrating situation you see that everyone is being treated the same way, or by some reasonable standard, you are less likely to act aggressively than if you feel you have been singled out or given less favorable treatment than others. A rationing system used during the Second World War equalized the discomfort resulting from deprivation and made it easier for people to accept "doing without."

There are, of course, instances where individuals do not see themselves as relatively deprived, but almost everyone involved sees themselves as deprived. The rules, the regime, the school policy, the employer—the system itself—is seen as unfair to almost all. As we shall see in our chapter on community violence, this can be a key ingredient in a recipe for a riot, if not an insurrection. A story cited by Brenda Bredemeier and David Shields makes this point quite well.[21] The incident that happened at Roosevelt Raceway in New York has the flavor of a Damon Runyon story. During one of the races, an accident caused six of the eight horses not to finish the race. Now, the rules of the race track then in force required the judge to declare the race had been run—the race was declared official. All of the people who bet on the six horses involved in the accident lost their money. Perceiving these rules as utterly unfair, these bettors reacted with violence. They attacked the judge's booth, smashed the tote board and damaged the automobiles in the parking lot.

Heredity and Aggression

A successful Broadway play in the 1950s was called *The Bad Seed*. The title of the play conveys the idea of someone being born bad; that the antisocial, unacceptable behaviors that would be portrayed on the stage were almost predetermined by the person's genetic makeup. A contrasting point of view was suggested by another theatrical title—this one a film from the 1930s—*They Made Me a Criminal*. The implication of this title was that environmental forces impinged on the individual, turning an otherwise good person to a life of crime.

These polar-opposite titles raise the time-honored question of heredity versus environment—sometimes stated as nature versus nurture, this time focused on aggression.

The methods used by researchers to try to disentangle the effects of heredity and environment are twin studies and adoption studies. In twin studies, monozygotic (MZ) twins, which are also called identical twins, are compared with dizygotic (DZ) twins which are also called fraternal twins. MZ twins share 100 percent of their genes; their heredity is identical. DZ twins share the same percent of their genes (on average 50 percent) as any other pairs of siblings. If aggressiveness has a genetic basis, we would expect to find MZ twins more alike on measures of aggressiveness than DZ twins.

Most of the research that bears on this question was carried out on incarcerated criminals, which limits our ability to generalize when we consider aggressiveness in the overall population. In a review of these studies, Lisbeth DiLalla and Irving Gottesman noted that the concordance rates for criminal offenses were much higher for MZ twins than for DZ twins, suggesting that a tendency toward criminality is inherited.[22] Interestingly though, the concordance rates for non-violent criminals was higher than it was for violent criminals, not what you would expect to find if you were looking for pure genetic effects for aggression. Attempts to apply the twin study method to younger persons who have been arrested (delinquents) have found little difference between MZ and DZ twins. DiLalla and Gottesman observed, "The fact that the DZ twin concordance is so high suggests a very strong environmental effect."[23]

The rationale for adoption studies is that children who are adopted at birth or shortly thereafter bring into their new homes a different hereditary makeup from the members of their adopted families. Now, if it happens that a biological parent is a criminal and the child develops into a criminal in this new environment in which there are no criminals, one would strongly suspect a hereditary influence. Conversely, in the case where the biological parents have no criminal record while it turns out there are criminals in the new home, if the child develops criminal tendencies one would suspect environmental influences. Studies conducted on adoptees by Cloninger and his colleagues pointed to both hereditary and environmental influences.[24] When neither biological nor adopted parents or relatives were criminals, the child had only a slight chance of developing into a criminal (three percent). When biological parents were criminals but adoptive parents were not, the number rose to 12 percent. When both biological and adoptive parents were criminals, 40 percent of the children became criminals. DiLalla and Gottesman concluded that there was "a multiplicative or truly interactional effect of both genetic and environmental influences ... when both were combined they greatly increased the risk of later criminality."[25] While criminality is clearly not a pure measure of aggressiveness, the results of adoption studies are consistent with those of the twin studies in indicating some hereditary influence in becoming a criminal.

In a recent paper, Donna Miles and Gregory Carey revisited the question, looking at some studies that used more pure measures of aggression. These studies indicated that heredity played a substantial role in self-reports of aggressive tendencies. Miles and Carey concluded that heredity might account for as much as 50 percent of the variance.[26] It seems likely that both genetic and environmental factors play important roles in aggressiveness.

Gender Differences in Aggressiveness

When one observes toddlers, one sees little difference between boys and girls in aggressiveness. By the early years of elementary school, however, boys are more likely to be aggressive—particularly physically aggressive—than girls and this gender difference persists into adulthood.[27] Men score higher than women on both verbal and physical aggression scales of the Aggression Questionnaire devised by Buss and Perry.[28] Men are much more likely than women to be arrested for violent crimes. Ann Bettencourt and Norman Miller reviewed 64 experimental studies in which researchers looked at gender and aggressiveness.[29] Using the statistical procedure meta-analysis to see if there was an overall statistical difference in these studies between the sexes, Bettencourt and Miller found a clear gender difference for aggressiveness. The difference was largest when there was no provocation used in the experiment. When women were provoked in a study, the differences between men and women in aggressiveness were greatly reduced. In fact, in a recent study carried out by Joseph Mikolic and his colleagues, women responded with more verbal aggression than men to perceived unfairness that impacted them personally.[30] Interestingly, a group solely composed of women reacted more aggressively to such provocation than a group solely composed of men. The study suggests that when women perceive the breaking of an implied social contract that they will be treated fairly, their reaction can be as aggressive as men's, if not more so.

When we consider minor acts of aggression, there is a gender reversal. For young adults, at least, it is the female of the species who is somewhat more likely to flail away at her male partner with angry words and deeds than the reverse. The world's literature has given us our share of angry women (e.g., Medea, Lady Macbeth, Kathryn in *The Taming of the Shrew*) but recent research findings may still seem surprising. In a study reported by Lynn Magdol and her colleagues, nearly a thousand young adults (age 21) were questioned both about being aggressive with their partners and about being victims of partner aggression.[31] The young women in the sample were more likely to dish out aggressive acts and less likely to receive them. Here are a few statistics from the study for carrying out aggressive acts.

- Insulting or swearing: women 67 percent, men 53 percent
- Sulking or refusing to talk: women 60 percent, men 52 percent
- Threatening to hit or throw: women 24 percent, men 10 percent
- Pushing, grabbing, shoving partner: women 29 percent, men 21 percent
- Slapping partner: women 19 percent, men 6 percent[32]

The researchers observed, "The present study indicates that at least as many women as men are violent toward their partners. These results corroborate previous surveys of community samples in the United States."[33]

The researchers felt that their findings were counterintuitive and wondered what accounted for them. Some of their speculations are interesting. They noted that men and women may differ in their expectations about the consequences of physical violence. "Men may understand that the likelihood is very high that they will injure their partner or be prosecuted and therefore, men perceive strong reasons to constrain their assaultive behavior. Men's partners are generally younger and weaker, and men's socialization reinforces the rule to restrain violence against targets who are weaker than themselves.... In direct contrast, women may understand that the likelihood is very low that they will injure their partner or be prosecuted. Their partners are generally older and stronger; given social norms constraining men's behavior toward women, women may also anticipate that few men will hit back."[34]

There are subtle forms of aggression in interpersonal relationships that are also more likely to be employed by females than males. Think of such behaviors as gossiping, character defamation, betraying trust, attempts to exclude people from groups and threatening to withhold friendship and affection. For these subtle forms of aggression, the perpetrator doesn't hit anybody, doesn't need to confront the target person, and in fact may leave no fingerprints on the aggressive deed. These forms of relational and indirect social aggression are observable by the middle to later years of elementary school. School children seem able to pick out their classmates who are victims of relational aggression, just like they are able to pick out those who are victims of overt physical aggression. Using a peer nomination technique, Nicki Crick and Maureen Bigbee asked fourth and fifth graders to check off the names of their classmates who were left out at play because one of their friends was mad at them or who were the targets of lies so other kids wouldn't like them.[35] The peer nominations revealed that while victims of overt aggression (e.g., Who gets beat up? Who gets picked on?) were almost always boys, victims of relational aggression were usually girls. Victims of physical aggression and relational aggression both reacted with emotional distress and loneliness.

The Testosterone Connection

When there is physical violence that is severe enough to cause physical injury, the male is usually the perpetrator. In shelters, one finds battered wives, not battered husbands. What accounts for this tendency to let fists fly? Researchers have looked at both biological and social factors. The prime suspect among biological factors is the sex hormone testosterone. There is considerable evidence that testosterone plays a role in male aggressiveness. In comparing violent and nonviolent male offenders, researchers have found higher levels of testosterone in the violent offenders.[36] In a study carried out on more than 4,000 veterans, serum testosterone was related to being assaultive toward other people.[37] In studies of university students, testosterone was related to scores on aggression questionnaires.[38]

Testosterone levels are affected by participating in competitive contact sports such as hockey or wrestling.[39] In an interesting experiment, Brian Gladue found that testosterone levels rose in participants in a competitive computer-driven reaction time task.[40] In the experimental situation, two young men faced a computer monitor with a wooden panel separating them. As the men watched the monitor, they first saw the word "wait." Next, the word "ready" appeared. A few seconds later, the word "go" appeared. At this signal, each man was supposed to press a button set 40 centimeters directly in front of him as quickly as he could. The winner of each trial was the one who pressed the button first. At the end of each trial the winner was announced. The overall winner was declared at the end of the trials. In reality, the contest was rigged. Neither contestant could see what the other was doing, and winners and losers were determined ahead of time by the experimenters. Subjects were randomly assigned to be: (1) decisive winners; (2) close winners; (3) close losers; and (4) decisive losers. Before, during and after the contest, testosterone levels were assessed by collecting salivary samples that were subsequently analyzed in the laboratory.

The results showed that the testosterone levels of the subjects rose during the competition, which indicates that competition in men need not be physical nor even involve exertion to raise testosterone levels. When it's simply "me against you," or one might assume by extension "us against them," testosterone levels rise. The fact of winning also influenced testosterone levels. Testosterone levels were higher in winners than losers for a period of time after the competition was over. One wonders whether these extended hormonal effects have anything to do with the fists-in-the-air, jumping around theatrics of some professional football players after making a good play, such as sacking the quarterback—a kind of post-win ceremony of elation.

Gladue and his colleagues stress the fact that the contestants in their experiment never actually won the competition—they just thought they won. The belief of victory altered hormone levels.

The relation of testosterone to aggression seems more equivocal in women than in men. Some researchers have reported that testosterone levels are related to aggression in women paralleling the findings for men.[41] However, a 1991 study reported by Gladue found that while testosterone levels tended to be higher in aggressive than nonaggressive men, he found the opposite pattern for women.[42] This study leaves the issue of the relation of testosterone and aggression in women an open question.

J. Van Goozen and his colleagues have reported some intriguing results from studies of individuals who have undergone sex changes.[43] They reported that when female-to-male transsexuals were given testosterone, their levels of self-reported anger and aggression proneness increased. When male-to-female transsexuals were given estrogens and anti-testosterone drugs, their self-report levels of anger and aggression-proneness decreased. Such studies tend to confirm the role of testosterone in aggression.

Leaving aside testosterone levels, Gladue looked at levels of aggression in people who were gay and lesbian.[44] In one of two studies, he found that homosexual men were less physically aggressive on self-report scales than heterosexual men. In regard to lesbians,

Gladue reported that they appeared no more physically aggressive than their heterosexual counterparts, which contradicts a stereotype that lesbians are more male-like in their behavior than heterosexual women. In one of his studies, lesbians were actually less physically aggressive than heterosexual women.

The Serotonin Connection

Serotonin is one of the chemical neurotransmitters that permit the transmission of information in the brain and nervous system. Among neurotransmitters, serotonin has become a kind of gold nugget for researchers because serotonin abnormalities have been linked to important emotional disorders such as depression and allied behaviors such as suicide. Researchers have now provided preliminary evidence that implicates serotonin in aggressive behavior.[45]

Studies of serotonin levels and aggressive behavior have been carried out now for about 20 years. The studies have used psychiatric interviews, experimental procedures to raise aggression levels and populations who have been demonstrably aggressive—men who committed or attempted to commit murder. A variety of methods have been used to assess serotonin levels including concentration of a major metabolite (5-HIAA) of serotonin in cerebrospinal fluid, and hormonal (prolactin) response to pharmacochallenge. Although there are inconsistencies in the research reported, it looks as if serotonin functioning is associated with aggressive behavior. While it is not yet clear whether serotonin levels bear a cause-and-effect relation to aggressive behavior, the possibilities for treating some types of aggressive behavior with drugs that will influence serotonin levels offers interesting possibilities for research. Indeed, in a recent study, Emil Coccaro and Richard Kavoussi evaluated the effectiveness of fluoxetine hydrochloride, a drug that is a selective serotonin-reuptake inhibitor, on patients who were not depressed but had a substantial history of "impulsive aggressive" behavior.[46] Compared to a group of patients receiving a placebo, the group receiving fluoxetine evidenced a reduction in impulsive aggressive behavior. The results are, to say the least, interesting.

Aggression as Retaliation

It happened in the waiting room of an allergist. A mother was reading a magazine while her two very small children were playing with toys on the floor near her. One toddler was playing with a toy truck when his brother pushed her out of the way and seized the truck for himself. She shoved him right back and went after the truck. Her reaction was quick. Whatever thought processes were involved in her decision to retaliate took place quickly. It was an instant response.

By striking back, the toddler in the physician's office had regained her toy. Her chastised brother left her alone. It doesn't always work out this way. The brother could have resumed his assault on his sister, seizing the toy and inflicting pain in the process. His sister could have learned that she was overmatched and couldn't win the contest. A dominance relationship might have been established in which all she could do was to concede and withdraw. Naturalists have observed dominance hierarchies in a number of mammals where brute force establishes rights and privileges. In the case of the toddler, however, there would have been an arbitrator to appeal to: Mother. She appears all-powerful and an appeal can put a quick end to her brother's bullying. Mother's ability to retaliate can be a clear and present deterrent.

Our definition of an aggressive act is one that is intended to inflict harm. As such, striking out in self-defense or in retaliation is still an aggressive act, although there is clearly a distinction both in law and in custom between unprovoked and provoked aggression. Self defense is a time-honored justification for acts of violence in a court of law. The threat of retaliation is one way of keeping the peace. There was a long-running television commercial for martial arts training in which a child says, "Nobody bothers me." It was the prospect of massive retaliation that prevented a nuclear war during the bitterest days of the cold war between the NATO Alliance and the Soviet Union. A credible threat of retaliation may inhibit aggression both on the levels of individuals and nation states.

The willingness to strike back, however, presents an ethical dilemma for some people as violence of any kind is proscribed by their religious teachings. This is clearly not the case for all ethical systems. The laws of the ancient Hebrews based on earlier Babylonian models sanctioned retaliation. What could be more explicit and measured than "an eye for an eye and a tooth for a tooth"? The Koran permits retaliation. In the Sermon on the Mount, however, Jesus offered a doctrine of turning the other cheek when affronted, not an easy thing to do for those who would follow his teachings in a competitive and sometimes combative world.

CHAPTER 3

Culture and Aggression

T he culture in which one lives influences the types of situations
that elicit angry feelings, whether such anger is expressed in the
form of aggressive acts and the way people respond to aggressive
acts. Research suggests that in America, anger arises more often in
situations involving relationships than is true for Europeans or
Japanese. In Japan, interactions with strangers are a more frequent
source of angry feelings than is the case for Americans.[1] In a study
of children, American and Chinese children were asked to describe
the kinds of situations that made them feel angry. The Chinese children listed more such situations than the Americans.[2]

Societies vary considerably in the extent to which they sanction
the expression of anger and aggressive acts. Anthropologists have
provided us with a wealth of illustrations. Among the Kaluli people
of New Guinea, E.D. Schieffelin wrote that "When a man has
suffered wrong or loss ... he may stamp furiously up and down the
outside yard or inside hall of the long house yelling the particulars
of his injury for everyone to hear."[3] While in America, such behavior might be considered justification for a psychiatric examination,
among the Kaluli stamping and yelling arouse sympathetic attention
and support for redress of grievances.

Expression of anger by stamping and yelling is one thing.
Beheading someone is quite another. The Llongots of the Philippines

sometimes worked up a passion and fury and then went out in a group set on headhunting. When they found a victim, killed and beheaded him, they returned home, having purged themselves of their anger.[4]

A textbook example of an aggressive people are the Yanomamo, who live in the tropical forests on the border between Venezuela and Brazil. They live in small villages subsisting largely on plantains, large bananas they roast or boil. Napoleon Chagnon has studied these villages for a period of years and has subtitled his book about the Yanomamo *The Fierce People*.[5] The characterization seems well justified. Considerable fighting erupts within villages and frequent open warfare occurs between villages. Typically the fights within the village are about infidelity: one man trysting with another man's wife. The combatants often attack each other with ten-foot-long clubs. These clubs are flexible, heavy and deliver a terrible blow.[6] The fights are bloody and the tops of many of the men's heads are covered with long scars. Individual fights often degenerate into general melees in which many men take part.

Men from one village often raid other villages. The objective of the raid is to kill some of the enemy villagers and escape before being discovered. Sometimes the raids have the purpose of abducting women. The raiders paint their faces, legs and chests with masticated charcoal, equip themselves with bows and arrows and set off to fight. One village was raided about 25 times during a period of 15 months. Warfare between villages may persist for years. Chagnon noted that at least one-fourth of adult Yanomamo males die violently.

Peaceful Societies

Many societies offer a marked contrast to the violence of the Yanomamo. Anthropologists have identified a number of societies in which there appears to be very little violence and aggressiveness. Writing in the *Psychological Bulletin*, Bruce Bonta noted that about 40 societies have been identified as peaceful, "where people live with virtually no, or in some cases absolutely no recorded instances of violence." Here are a few of the examples that Bonta cited.[7]

The Batek, a people who live in the highlands of the Malay Peninsula, subsist by hunting and trading. Kirk and Karen Endicott studied the Batek, reporting that the Batek were peaceful, that they abhorred interpersonal violence.[8] Both Batek men and women lived free from threats of violence.

The Piaroa, a native people in Venezuela, lived until recently in forest villages in the Venezuelan highlands. In the 1970s they relocated to more permanent settlements. Spending more than a year with the Piaroa, Joanna Overing reported that life in the forest villages was almost completely free of violence.[9] Children, teenagers and adults did not express anger through physical acts. She reported that spouses and children were never struck and that the people were appalled by any display of aggression.

The Tahitians of Polynesia have long had a reputation as peaceful people. After living with the Tahitians for about two years, Robert Levy noted little conflict, open hostility or aggression on the islands.[10] The people were described as gentle, showing little anger towards one another. Children's play was characterized by minimal conflict and aggressiveness.

The Tristan Islanders live on a remote island near the nation of South Africa. The people fish and farm for a livelihood. During the 1940s Peter Munch lived with the Tristan Islanders for about a year. He reported that quarrels were rare.[11] The highest level of observed hostility on the island occurred when two people stopped talking to each other for a short period of time. Fights had not occurred in living memory.

The Ladakhis are Tibetan Buddhists who live in the high mountains of northern India. They are farmers and tend livestock. Living among the Ladakhis for many years, H. Norberg Hodge reported that aggressive acts and arguments were rare events.[12] Villagers said that they had no memory of fighting within the village.

Most of these examples of nonaggressive societies are relatively small communities of peoples who live in areas that seem remote to us. Their lives have been only marginally touched by the urban, technologically-based cultures that are increasingly dominating the planet. Yet even within the United States, some groups have sealed themselves off to a degree, establishing artificial boundaries between themselves and the main cultural stream. The Amish, Hutterites and Mennonites are illustrations of peoples who maintain relatively peaceful, non-aggressive traditions when compared to the overall American society. Among the Amish, for example, dramatic restrictions in aggressive behavior are maintained by early and consistent education discouraging aggression and by continuing social pressures.[13]

Social Class and Aggressiveness

Within the larger American society, we can observe differences in aggressive behavior, though not as dramatic as the difference between isolated cultures such as the Amish and the general population. Social class, or socio-economic status, a term preferred by researchers because it lends itself to more objective measurement, is related to acts of aggressive behavior. Middle class people tend to hold and promote values that put restraints on aggressive behaviors. Watching an aggressive football game is an acceptable, often valued activity among middle class men, but that's about where it's supposed to stop. It is unacceptable for these men to beat up their wives or children, and their children are not supposed to beat up each other or the neighbor's children. Such social restraints are less evident as one drops toward the bottom of the class structure, where one finds increases in the rates of family violence.[14]

An interesting study carried out in a small Southern city by Janis Kupersmidt and her colleagues highlights the restraining influence of middle class environments.[15] Kupersmidt's team studied more than a thousand second through fifth grade children. They made an assessment of how physically aggressive these children were by asking the children in their classrooms to nominate three classmates who fought a lot. A child who received a relatively large number of nominations was considered more aggressive than one who received relatively few nominations. The researchers found that black children living in low-income families headed by a single parent were the most aggressive children in their sample. However, when the researchers examined the census track showing where these children lived, they uncovered an interesting pattern. Black children from low-income, single-parent homes who lived in a middle class neighborhood were less aggressive than the black children from low-income, single-parent homes who lived in a lower class neighborhood. These low-income black children living in middle-class neighborhoods were not appreciably different from the other children in the study in terms of aggressiveness.

Reasons for Peaceful Societies

In his article on peaceful societies, Bonta took the position that economics is not the driving force behind the peacefulness of these societies. Rather than a model of economic determinism, Bonta sees values as the critical factor. Values can override a particular form of economic organization. "In any case, the reasons for the peacefulness in these societies transcend their economic organization. Peacefulness is an essential aspect of the worldviews, attitudes and beliefs of the nonviolent societies. From societies as diverse as the Amish, Semai, and Tristan Islanders, the peacefulness that they achieve is not due to their collective, or lack of collective, economic behavior but to their very strong beliefs in their need to be peaceful, and ... their psychological strategies that reinforce, strengthen, and cement those shared beliefs and attitudes into daily practices that work most, or in some cases all, of the time. Cooperation is more than just an economic consideration."[16]

While Bonta rejects economic determinism, he points out that most of these nonaggressive societies emphasize cooperation rather than competition and de-emphasize achievement. In examining the reports for 25 of these peaceful societies, he concluded that 23 emphasized cooperative rather than competitive behavior. These societies "shun competition as inimical to their beliefs and firmly link it with aggression and violence."[17] Bonta further notes, "There is no question that the peacefulness of these societies is dependent, in the minds of the peaceful peoples, on their opposition to competition."

Among the examples Bonta cites are the Ifaluk, a people who live by fishing and gardening on a small Pacific island in Micronesia. The Ifaluk are described as "placing a high value on helpfulness, sharing, and cooperation as part of their strongly felt ethic of nonaggression."[18] They value people who are calm and gentle, describing such people with the same word used to describe a calm lagoon. The Ifaluk strongly disapprove of displaying personal possessions and showing off.

Many of these peaceful societies that restrain and inhibit competition also discourage the recognition of individual achievement. Instead of recognizing individual achievement, they promote values of humility and modesty. In these societies, one would not find the equivalent of our gold stars for performing well at piano lessons,

"A" grades for solving the problems on a math test or trophies for winning a tennis match. In these societies, the appropriate response after a successful performance would be a modest disclaimer such as, "It was really nothing."

Acquisitiveness, Power and Aggression

Viewed through the eyes of the inhabitants of the small, peaceful communities we have discussed, achievement and competition are precursors of aggressiveness and violence. Their social theory, explicit or implicit, is that if they rein in individualistic aspirations, they will deter aggression. Acquisitiveness would seem to fit in the same mold. Desire for wealth would probably be seen as both bad for the individual and inimical to the interest of the community. The Amish of Lancaster County, Pennsylvania traditionally farmed for a living. In recent years, many of the Amish began to operate small businesses because there was not enough land available for everyone to farm. However, there is social pressure in the community not to allow these businesses to grow too large. As one businessman put it, his people (the Amish) would interpret too much growth as a sign of greed.[19]

Aggression in Nation States

The motivations for nations to fight one another have been many and varied. Wars have been fought for revenge of perceived injustices, because of ethnic hatreds, because a nation was simply obligated to join in a conflict to honor a treaty commitment, and for a range of political, economic and religious reasons. Religious zeal, for example, led to warfare between Christians and Muslims in the Crusades and was a factor in the devastating Thirty Years' War that ravaged Europe in the 17th century. Indeed, in her book *The First Salute*, historian Barbara Tuchman noted that intramural religious fights were the "most passionate and venomous of any."[20]

Granted the multiplicity of causes for warfare, the historical record will show that acquisitiveness has been one of the prime motivations for the aggressive acts of nation states and their precursors.

The prototype in both ancient and modern times is the thief who bludgeons his victim and steals his purse. Often coupled with the desire to possess more is another motivation, a desire to have power over others, to dominate. In theoretical schemes developed in psychology to describe personality needs, the need to dominate and the need for aggression are considered close neighbors.[21] To dominate, one often has to infringe into and diminish the space and prerogatives of others.

Organized mayhem for purpose of material gain is not unique to the human species. Some ants go on raiding expeditions to capture other ants for slaves. Chimpanzees, with whom the human species shares so much DNA, have been observed to systematically hunt down and destroy the males of a nearby community, then seize both their territory and their females. The long-time student of primate behavior in the wild, Jane Goodall, mused that if these chimpanzees had possessed firearms and knew how to use them, they might have used them to kill.[22]

The human record of instrumental aggression—raiding, killing and fighting territorial wars in the pursuit of material gain—dwarfs that of chimpanzees. It probably extends far into prehistory, long before humans invented cuneiform tablets to record their deeds.

Excavations from a neolithic agricultural settlement in northeastern Belgium that thrived some 7,000 years ago revealed evidence of sophisticated fortifications (deep ditches, timbered palisades) and pitched battles.[23] The skeletons in a cemetery included 30 bodies of men, women and children who had holes in their skulls probably caused by the blows of ax heads. The particulars surrounding these battles are of course unknown but it is believed that there was a conflict between people who foraged for subsistence and the farmers who were expanding their holdings. There is a parallel between this hypothesized scenario and the western expansion of the white man into the North American continent.

Even with the advent of historical documents and contemporaneous accounts, it is not always possible to attribute with certainty the aggressive acts of nation states to one or another motivation. Still, there are more than enough illustrations in the history of human conflict to suggest that acquisitiveness and power needs—sometimes one, sometimes the other, and sometimes both—play a role in unleashing aggressive acts. The history of the ancient world, the

Near East and Mediterranean—the cradle of Western civilization—provides a good beginning point for asserting that the aggressive acts of states are often based on acquisitiveness. Underlying much of the political history of this time was a simple idea: you have something we want, we'll take it. Acquisitiveness was the motivation, military power the means and if one needed an ethical justification for seizing the lands, goods and produce of another people, one could ascribe it to the wishes of their gods. The ancient Hebrews used the justification explicitly in seizing the lands of the Canaanites. Such niceties for justifying attacks on one's neighbors may have never occurred to the succession of empire builders—the Assyrians, Babylonians and Persians—whose rulers simply took everything they could get as a matter of course. The simple threat of invasion was often all that was needed. Submit (send us tokens of earth and water) or we will torch what you have and enslave the survivors. The Old Testament is replete with stories of people who fought back, lost and suffered the consequences. The story of the Lost Ten Tribes of Israel is a textbook example.

When the last and largest of the ancient empires—that of Rome—crumbled and Europe lapsed into what has been called the Dark Ages, the use of aggression in the pursuit of material gain hardly ceased. The epoch of Viking raids was a blatant example of unprovoked attacks in the pursuit of plunder.

The Spanish conquests in the New World in the 1500s are another good illustration of greed leading to aggression. Cortez, who conquered the Aztec Empire of Mexico, and Pizzaro, who emulated him with the Incas of Peru, were treasure hunters backed by an avaricious Spanish crown. Casualties among the native populations and enslavement of the indigenous people to work the gold mines were rationalized with the justification that the conquistadors brought with them priests who would convert the natives to Christianity.

The infamous African slave trade began in the wake of the Spanish conquests. The sugar plantations of the West Indies provided a lucrative income but required a constant supply of labor to work the fields. Mortality of the workers was high. Africans were thought to be more durable workers in this climate than Europeans or the native peoples and the slave trade boomed. Africans, Arabs and Europeans were all complicit in promoting raiding expeditions that captured, chained and deported Africans in thousands of voyages across the Atlantic. Some people became rich while many of the victims died. If a rationalization for this barbarism was needed, it was held that the Africans were inferior, even subhumans. So it really didn't matter what happened to them.

An impetus for the exploitive behavior of the Europeans during the 16th, 17th and 18th centuries was the economic philosophy of mercantilism. The theory held that the more riches—principally in the form of gold and other precious metals a nation could accrue within its borders—and the less money it had to let go of, the better off the nation would be. With this doctrine, it made sense to acquire colonies through settlement and military conquest, exploit the raw materials of these colonies, use slave labor when possible and force the colonies to buy the mother country's value-added manufactured products. In commenting about the European wars of the 18th century, including the failed British effort to hold on to the American colonies, Barbara Tuchman observed that material gain was the justification required for all of the war-like enterprises that were undertaken.

In succeeding centuries, seizure of most of Africa, much of the Middle East and Southeast Asia by European empire builders was propelled largely by acquisitiveness, intra–European competitiveness and dominance needs. One of the rationalizations that made these aggressive acts palatable to the conscience of Europeans was a racial one. It was said to be "the white man's burden" to civilize his less advanced (if not inferior) fellow man. Taking over other countries was for the other people's own good. Churning up the lives of the Africans, Arabs and Southeast Asians, the Europeans sought to convince themselves that they were doing the subjugated peoples a favor.

One of the more egregious accounts of 19th century European colonialism was the annexation of the Congo by Belgium's King Leopold II. In his book, *King Leopold's Ghost*, Adam Hochschild related how the king, desirous of acquiring an African colony to rival his larger neighbors, England, France and Germany, hired the renowned explorer Henry Morton Stanley to open up the vast territory of the Congo for exploitation.[24] Stanley traversed the Congo, acquiring the land through treaties with the native chiefs for their signatures (usually an X mark) on documents they couldn't read. The chiefs received, in Stanley's words, "an ample supply of fine clothes, flunkey coats and tinsel-braided uniforms."[25] Having obtained endorsement of the chiefs, Leopold obtained the endorsement of his fellow European heads of state at a conference held in Berlin. Leopold called his new colony a "Confederation of Free Negro Republics" that would exist under his "guidance."[26] With this euphemism Leopold's agents plundered the Congo with such brutality that it shocked the conscience of the Western world. The motivation underlying the abuse of the indigenous population of the Congo was the need for an economic payoff for Leopold's investment. The payoff came first in the form of ivory and then from rubber. Americans and Europeans had discovered many ways to use rubber—in rain coats, bicycle tires, tubes and insulation—and couldn't get enough of the substance to meet their needs. Leopold decided to make his fortune by filling this need. Wild rubber grew in vines in the rain forests of the Congo. A vast army of laborers was needed to harvest the rubber. However, the work meant traveling to distant, often waterlogged forests while the extrication of the rubber from the plant itself could be difficult and unpleasant. The natives were unwilling.

Leopold's agents forced the men to work by raiding their villages and taking their wives hostage. Hostage-taking was soon supplemented by outright killing as a means of intimidation. Leopold's enforcers sometimes cut off the hands of their victims and smoked them to preserve them as a way of keeping a body count to prove that they were doing their job. Diaries kept by some of Leopold's officers revealed that massacres in villages were commonplace events.[27]

When the atrocities in the Congo came to the attention of the outside world, there was great indignation. Among those who spoke out was the American writer Mark Twain. But before Leopold's "civilizing mission" in the Congo had run its course, very large numbers of the people had been murdered or died from starvation.

In many ways, the actions of the newly-independent United States were similar to those of the European powers. The Americans did not look abroad for foreign colonies; rather, they cast their eyes to the west, to the vast continent that stretched to the Pacific Ocean. Through much of the 19th century, the white population of the United States found an ever increasing need for land to cultivate and settle. The indigenous inhabitants were driven out of their villages and hunting grounds, forced ever westward and eventually into reservations. Again, it was the same general formula, acquisitiveness motives backed by military power and rationalized by an ideology that demonized the natives as savages. The Mexican War offered another example of a more powerful state seizing desirable lands from a weaker neighbor.

The Second World War provided yet more evidence of aggression in the pursuit of acquisitiveness and power. The Japanese needed raw materials including rubber and oil to fuel a developing empire. Their armies marched into Korea, Manchuria, China, Indonesia and Malaysia to get it. These conquests were punctuated with atrocities. In her book *The Rape of Nanking*, Iris Chang details glaring acts of savagery.[28] Included is a statement from Japanese military correspondent Yokio Omata who witnessed Chinese prisoners lined up along the river. He wrote that the prisoners in the first row were beheaded while those in the second row were forced to dump the severed bodies into the river before being beheaded themselves. The slaughter went on nonstop throughout the day.[29]

The civilian population fared little better. Chang tells the fascinating story of John Rabe, a German businessman who lived in Nanking. Although an enthusiastic member of the Nazi party, he was appalled by the Nanking atrocities and became "the Oskar Schindler of China." He and other members of the foreign national community set up a safety zone that saved thousands of people. In a report to, of all people, Adolph Hitler, Rabe described the epidemic of rapes in the city. He wrote that the Japanese raped the women and girls and killed anyone who offered resistance. The rape victims included girls under the age of eight and women over the age of 70. After being raped, the women were brutally knocked down and beaten up.[30] When Rabe returned to Germany and spoke about the Nanking massacres, he was arrested by the Gestapo and warned not to talk about Nanking again. The number of fatalities inflicted by the Japanese in Nanking in a few weeks' time was estimated to be more than 260,000.

Adolph Hitler cast his eyes east at Russia with the notion of turning the area into a breadbasket for Germany. With his ideology that the German people constituted a master race and that Slavs were expendable, he cared little that millions of Russians would be slaughtered in the process. Like the earlier Japanese invasion of China, the Nazi European conquests were coupled with brutality.

Hitler's ultimate horror, the Holocaust, was unprecedented both in its scope and the cold-blooded way it was carried out.

Perhaps the most blatant example of cross-border aggressiveness in the pursuit of riches since the Second World War was Iraq's invasion of Kuwait. Oil-rich Kuwait was a tempting target for the ambitious dictator Saddam Hussein. An unopposed military takeover also offered the possibility of hegemony in the Persian Gulf states. It was his misfortune that the leaders of the West had too vivid a memory of the consequences of appeasing Hitler in the 1930s to allow his invasion to stand, and drove his army out of Kuwait.

These sorry chapters in human history raise many questions and perhaps most troubling among them is, why did the people in the aggressor nations countenance and support these acts? When the country's ruler had near absolute power, the people had little choice. In the empires of the ancient world, in Nazi Germany and in contemporary Iraq to raise dissident voices could be a perilous act. Speaking out could lead to imprisonment or death.

When one considers a government that was accountable to the people via elections or was even subject to minimal checks and balances, the answer to the question becomes more complex. Ideology seems to be one factor. Believing that the acquisition of foreign territories is justified by "manifest destiny," as was once true for the United States, or by supposed superiority of culture and civilization, as was true for the European powers, could go a long way towards justifying aggressive intervention. Such beliefs might have provided a plausible basis for believing that what the nation was doing was morally defensible, even laudable, while turning a blind eye to the huge profits from such enterprises as West Indies sugar plantations and the diamond mines of southern Africa.

Going beyond the relatively benign justification of *noblesse oblige* is a belief system that holds that there is glory in foreign conquest. Both the French Foreign Legion of the 1920s and 1930s and the "thin red line" of soldiers who for many years helped hold the far-flung British Empire together are the stuff of which legends and some terrific movies were made. Film buffs will recall *Beau Geste* and *Gunga Din*. Who could have rooted for the natives when Gary Cooper and Cary Grant were holding down the fort for the empire? Perhaps it was the Romans who carried the glorification of foreign conquest to an extreme by staging "triumphs" for their conquering generals and legions. It would take Hollywood with a cast of thousands to recreate these events. The Romans really knew how to humiliate their victims; in the grand procession, the chained prisoners marched behind a yoke.

In trying to understand why the German people followed Hitler into aggressive conquest and ultimately into an abyss and why Japanese soldiers rarely surrendered, choosing to fight to the death, social scientists in the 1940s explored the possibility that there was something in the national character of these peoples that made such behavior possible. These speculations received a boost at the time from the popularity of Ruth Benedict's book, *Patterns of Culture,* in which she seemed able to paint entire cultures with broad brushes using such terms as "Dionysian" (frenzied, seeking excess) and "Apollonian" (ordered, measured).[31]

If such characterizations could be applied to American Indian peoples, why not take a crack at the Germans and Japanese? To make the question even more enticing, why not apply psychoanalytic concepts relating to child-raising (which were in vogue at the time) and tie the whole thing up in a neat package? Could German militarism be related to an authoritarian nuclear family? Could Japanese fanaticism be explained by harsh toilet training practices?

In an article written during the Second World War, Geoffrey Gorer emphasized the role of toilet training in forming Japanese character and Ruth Benedict shortly afterwards echoed the theme in her book, *The Chrysanthemum and the Sword.*[32] She wrote, "What the baby learns from this implacable training prepares him to accept in adulthood the subtler compulsions of Japanese culture."[33] Gorer and Benedict were pushing the envelope, making inquiries and inferences beyond what the state of the arts in their disciplines could reasonably justify. Now, a half-century later, both German and Japanese militarism have receded to unpleasant memories. Has the national character of these people changed, making this possible? Or was national character not a reasonable place to look for explanations in the first place? The more likely explanation for these changes is that the political institutions in both countries changed from authoritarian to democratic. It is harder to sell people in democracies on the need for extra-territorial wars than in tightly controlled societies.

Ethno-national Conflicts

In the waning years of the 20th century such factors as the threat of nuclear destruction, the development of collective security arrangements and the growing interdependence of the world's economies has led to a diminution of cases of cross-border aggression committed by one nation state against another. In its place, however, we have witnessed an increase in ethnic conflicts within the same country. A partial list of nations that have experienced such internal conflicts includes Northern Ireland, Bosnia, Georgia, Turkey, Sudan, Rwanda, Afghanistan, Tadzhikistan and Sri Lanka. These "enthno-national" conflicts typically contain "us versus them" elements. Our fighters are heroic; yours are terrorists. Each group believes its cause is just and demonizes the other group. The difficulties arise in that both groups share the same land and they can't get away from each other, even for a while. The conflicts tend to be protracted and vicious.

Although group identity is paramount in these conflicts, the old nemeses—acquisitiveness and dominance—are often elements in the picture. There is usually more to the conflict than the fact that two groups are simply culturally distinct.

In writing about the Israeli-Palestinian conflict, Nadim Rouhana and Daniel Bar-tal noted that such conflicts involve control over "vital tangible resources."[34] It is difficult to imagine peaceful coexistence when one ethnic group is the haves and the other ethnic group is the have-nots. The situation becomes even more difficult when public policy in the nation provides economic opportunities for one group and not for the other. The perception of fairness—the so-called level playing field—is probably of bedrock importance if there is going to be any chance of bridging the linguistic, religious and traditional differences that divide ethnic groups within a nation and allow them to share a common land and nationality. The alternative of splitting the planet into hundreds of more-or-less ethnically pure subdivisions is a geopolitical nightmare.

American Culture and Violence

Modern, technologically advanced societies differ appreciably in terms of the level of violence that takes place within them. Our

American society, which is second to none in its abundance, is also second to none among modern industrialized states in the rate of reported homicides. The Department of Justice noted that "From the Civil War to the present, 567,000 Americans have died in combat; but since 1920, over one million American citizens have been killed by firearms."[35]

In their book on crime and violence, Franklin Zimring and Gordon Hawkins presented statistical data suggesting that the rate of overall crime in the United States is not that out-of-line with other industrialized countries.[36] The crime rate here may seem uncomfortably high but it doesn't dwarf that of other countries. As the Justice Department's statement suggests, where we stand head and shoulders above the other nations is the homicide rate.

Zimring and Hawkins present some interesting comparisons. Los Angeles, California and Sydney, Australia both have populations of about 3.6 million. During 1992 Sydney experienced somewhat more burglaries (breaking and entering with intent to steal) than Los Angeles. However, there were only 53 homicides reported in Sydney while Los Angeles had more than 1,000.[37]

A comparison between New York City and London, England—both with populations in the seven million range—shows the same pattern; London had more theft and burglary than New York City but the homicide rate in New York City was ten times greater than in London.[38]

The authors observed that "The United States has about the same rate of crime and prevalence of criminality as the Netherlands and Australia. But ours is by far the most dangerous country to live in. We currently have a Netherlands-size crime problem and a king-size violence problem."[39]

Particularly troubling is the high rate of homicides committed by juveniles. Writing in a 1990 issue of the *Journal of the American Medical Association*, I.A. Fingerhut and J.C. Kleinman reported that the U.S. homicide rate of males 15 to 24 years was nearly 22 deaths per 100,000 population.[40] That was more than four times as high as the next highest country—Scotland. Our youth homicide rates were more than 20 times higher than one finds in Japan or Austria.

While violent crime is most noticeably a problem in our urban areas, particularly the inner cities, our well-to-do suburbs do not escape its reach. One summer day, I browsed through the weekly section of the newspaper that presented crime reports of a well-to-do suburban Maryland county. Here were three incidents that caught my eye:

July 22. A man shot another man during an argument. A 19-year-old man was arrested on the following day, charged with attempted first-degree murder.

July 28. A traffic argument began at a major intersection. The two drivers then drove to a nearby school parking lot. In the ensuing confrontation, one man, age 19, stabbed the other with a knife.

July 30. A panhandler stopped a passerby and asked him if he could borrow some money. The passerby said no. The panhandler stabbed him in the stomach.[41]

In two of these three incidents, the assailant was still in his teens. Although rates for violent crime have dropped significantly during the 1990s, the level of juvenile violence remains a worrisome problem. A 1989 national survey of more than 11,000 eighth and tenth graders found that a substantial number of young people have been involved in, or been victims of, violence. Nearly four out of ten had been involved in physical fights. One out of three had been threatened with bodily harm and 15 percent had been robbed.[42]

Youth violence that occurs with such frequency in American society rises to very high levels in our inner cities. Some of these areas have been referred to as "war zones." Statistics compiled in 1987 indicated that the homicide rates for black males between 15 and 24 years of age was seven times higher than was the case for white males in the same age group.[43] Much of this difference seems attributable to young blacks living in the inner cities.

Children who grow up in the inner cities of America learn that violence in their communities is a tangible reality. Violent acts are not the remote possibilities envisioned by people growing up in the suburbs. Inner city youngsters will probably observe or fall victim to violent acts at one time or another. Writing in the *American Psychologist*, Joy Osofsky summarized some of the research that documents this reality:

> The high rates of exposure to violence for children growing up
> in some inner-city neighborhoods with pervasive violence has been

well documented. In a survey of 6th, 8th, and 10th graders in New Haven in 1992, 40 percent reported witnessing at least one violent crime in the past year ... and almost all 8th graders knew someone who had been killed.[44]

Referring to a 1991 study carried out in a violence-prone African-American neighborhood in Chicago, Osofsky wrote, "One third of all school-age children had witnessed a homicide and that two thirds had witnessed a serious assault."[45]

Osofsky cited additional studies carried out in low-income neighborhoods in Washington, D.C. and New Orleans. "Fifty-one percent of the New Orleans fifth graders and 32% of the Washington, D.C. children had been victims of violence. Ninety-one percent of the children in New Orleans and 72% of those in Washington, D.C. had witnessed some type of violence."[46]

The most recent study I have seen was carried out by Albert Farrell and Steven Bruce in a large city in the Southeastern United States.[47] Questionnaire-type measures were administered at several points in time to children in urban public schools. Almost all of the children (94 percent) identified themselves as African American. The children were asked about their exposure to violence.

Here are some of the statistics reported for the boys. At one time or another, 24 percent reported that someone had threatened to shoot them, 37 percent had been beaten up, 42 percent had seen someone getting shot, 92 percent had seen someone getting arrested and almost all (96 percent) had heard the sounds of gunfire. The girls in the sample were less likely to report instances of personal threat. Eleven percent had been threatened that they would be shot and 16 percent had been beaten up.[48] But like the boys, almost all had witnessed arrests and had heard gunshots.

Structural Problems in Urban Areas

Even a cursory analysis suggests some of the economic and social factors that promote the level of violence in our inner cities. Broken families, lack of job opportunities and inadequate schools are basic structural conditions in many inner cities. These may be compounded by the presence of youth gangs, drug markets and the proliferation of weapons.

In describing the structural characteristics of urban neighborhoods, social scientists may utilize demographic data. Abraham Wandersman and Maury Nation pointed out a number of demographic
characteristics that seem to underlie high rates of social problems
such as child abuse and juvenile delinquency. These include "the percentage of residents living below poverty, the distribution of ethnic
characteristics, the percentage of families with high risk characteristics (e.g. female-headed households, single parents) and the rate of
population turnover in a given neighborhood."[49] Wandersman and
Nation noted that data collected as early as the 1920s showed that
"The numbers of juvenile arrests and court appearances were higher
in neighborhoods where there were large numbers of poor and
minority families and in neighborhoods where there were high rates
of turnover among the residents."[50] Observing that more recent
research has continued to confirm this pattern, they noted that "Factors such as the number of families in poverty, the level of cultural
heterogeneity, the number of divorced adults, the number of female-
headed households, and similar neighborhood indicators are predictors of more severe outcomes such as personal crimes and juvenile
violence."[51]

The Gang Culture

Youth gangs are not a new phenomena. Hollywood made films
featuring the *Dead End Kids* in the 1930s and a film, *City Across
the River*, based on the novel *The Amboy Dukes* in the postwar
years. Gang membership today appears to be growing. The percentage of students reporting street gang presence at school nearly
doubled between 1989 and 1995.[52] Typically gangs have names and
recognizable symbols. Sometimes gang insignia are etched as graffiti
on buildings in the neighborhood, and when the territory is in dispute, the insignia of the gangs may be overlaid, one upon the other.
    Some gangs are involved in drug trafficking. Gang membership
is a risk factor for violence. During a three-year period in Chicago
(1987 to 1990), more than 17,000 criminal offenses were classified
by the police as gang-related. Included in these offenses were 288
homicides and more than 800 violent assaults.[53]
    In a major urban area such as Chicago, one does not find a

monolithic gang structure; rather, there are different gangs in different neighborhoods. In a study of Chicago street gangs, Carolyn and Richard Block reported that there are about 40 major gangs in the city. Among the largest of these gangs are the Black Gangster Disciples Nation, which is most active in the south side of the city; the Latin Disciples; the Latin Kings and the Vice Lords, which is most active in the west side of the city. These four gangs have about 19,000 members in total.

Conflicts about control of territory are likely to, and do, arise when much of the city is turned into a patchwork of gangs. Gang violence tends to occur in certain neighborhoods of the city, which have been called "hot spots." In some hot spots, the homicide rate runs high. In the Chicago neighborhood of Pilsen, there were 48 homicides in a square mile during a three-year period.

In Chicago, gang-related homicides were not continuous; they tended to occur in spurts. For example, in the year 1965, there were 11 gang-motivated homicides. A few years later, in 1970, there were 70. The spurt in deaths reflected gang wars. Guns are used in almost all gang-related homicides, and increasingly, the guns used are automatic and semi-automatic weapons.

While some of the lethal gang violence in Chicago was instrumental in motivation—disputes concerning control over the lucrative drug trade—the lion's share of the violence had more to do with squabbles relating to turf and intra-gang and inter-gang issues. The Blocks noted that "Street gang-motivated violence often contains many expressive aspects—such as impulsive and emotional defense of one's identity as a gang member, defense and glorification of the reputation of the gang and gang members."[54] Even disputes about turf were not typically based on economic reasons.

A disquieting reality of inner city life is the availability of guns. In the way of perspective, a national survey of youth in grades six to 12 found that 59 percent of the children surveyed said that they could "get a handgun if they wanted."[55] More importantly, 15 percent of the students reported that they had actually carried a handgun in the last month. High as these national figures may seem, they are low compared to those reported in the inner cities. A 1993 study of seventh grade boys in an inner-city school found that 23 percent carried guns. For eighth graders, the figure had risen to 40 percent.[56]

What kind of children own guns? The Justice Department noted that "Handguns are more likely to be owned by socially maladjusted youth, dropouts, drug dealers, and individuals with a prior record of violent behavior."[57] Moreover, gun carrying at an inner-city school was associated with having been arrested, knowing victims of violence, starting fights and willingness to justify shooting someone. In 1992, 85 percent of the homicide victims in the 15- to 19-year age range were killed by guns.[58]

The Roll of the Slain

A symbolic act carried out in Washington, D.C., conveys the horror and bewilderment that may be lost in the recitation of statistics. In this symbolic act, students set up a lectern in a tent on the grass of George Washington University Hospital, which is not very far from the White House. The students took turns stepping to the lectern to read the names of people shot to death in the city in the preceding year.[59] It is solemn reading that takes time because the victims number in the hundreds. These are the names of people, each with his or her own story, survived by friends and family, that shared a common fate: being gunned down in an American city.

The Psychological Impact of Violence

Many children in the inner cities seem to become enured to the violence that sporadically erupts around them. Some of these children seem to become desensitized; studies suggest that they are not noticeably depressed. Research carried out by Lorion and Saltzman found that fifth and sixth grade children who lived in a crime-ridden neighborhood where they witnessed shootings, police raids— even a corpse—thought of these incidents as "nothing special."[60]

While desensitization may be taking place as a defensive coping mechanism, many of the youngsters nonetheless pay a psychological price for being immersed in this environment. They report symptoms that resemble post traumatic stress symptoms that soldiers may experience after combat and civilians may report after living through a natural disaster such as a flood or an earthquake. The psychiatric criteria for post traumatic stress disorder (PTSD) include nightmares, intrusive thoughts about the traumatic incidents and avoidance of situations that remind the individual about the incidents. The harsher the environment soldiers fight in, the more likely these symptoms will arise. However, it should be noted that even soldiers engaged in peacekeeping operations in potentially dangerous areas may develop these symptoms; researchers reported that about eight percent of the veterans of the Somalia operation met psychiatric criteria.[61]

Judging from research reports, PTSD symptoms appear to be fairly common among children who live in urban war zone environments. Studying African American children who lived in central city housing communities in a Southern city, Kevin Fitzpatrick and Janet Boldizar concluded that most of the children had experienced some post traumatic stress symptoms.[62] As is true for soldiers, the greater the exposure to violence, the greater the likelihood of PTSD symptoms.

Life After Homicide—Some Reactions of New York City Teenagers

When a teenager is murdered in the streets of our cities, the story typically makes the newspaper. Television camera crews may take a shot of the victim's apartment building and neighbors may be interviewed. Then the story disappears from public notice almost as quickly as it burst upon the scene. Fifteen minutes of tragic notoriety.

Many of the victims in these fleeting stories have brothers and sisters who live in the wake of murder. What happens to them psychologically? A team of psychiatrists at Columbia University interviewed 15 children about five months after the murder of an older sibling. While the sample is small, the team's observations are compelling.[63]

• Compared to a control group of young children who had not experienced such a tragedy, the bereaved children had more psychiatric disorders. The research team reported that 80 percent of these children had developed psychiatric disorders after the murder.

Symptoms included those of post traumatic stress disorder, anxiety and depression.

• The brothers and sisters of the murdered teenager experienced unresolved grief. They missed their dead siblings intensely.

• Some of the children tried not to think about the murder. They avoided reminders of the event. One 14-year-old boy stated that it had only sunk in a little bit that his brother was dead. He liked to think of his brother as if he were away at school. A teenage girl remarked that she gave away all of her necklaces because her brother had worn them.

• Some of the children feared that they, themselves, might be the targets of the same killer. They hesitated to go anywhere besides school or work.

Why so much violence in America, a land of plenty and opportunity? Some explanations for the high levels of violence focus on our economic system, others on our values. Marxian oriented theorists point to the American economic system, arguing that the level of violence is a consequence of insufficiently restrained capitalism. David Gil, who teaches social work at Brandeis University and acts as co-chair of the Socialist Party, USA, argued that violence is predictable in a society in which people exploit other people in the pursuit of social and economic gain.[64] In Gil's scenario, people who are exploited eventually react with counterviolence that often expresses itself in domestic violence, suicide and crime. The dominating classes respond to counterviolence that is perceived as threatening with additional repressive measures to maintain their advantage. One thinks of building more prisons to control crime. There are clear examples of what Gil is talking about in the struggles of the labor movement in the pre–World War II era. Miners working in unsafe conditions organized, struck and were met by police and troops. Guns were fired and people were bloodied in the struggle to unionize the Ford Motor Company.

Such incidents are a part of our history. Still, one sees little like this today. It can be argued that Gil's formulation has some application to incidents of police brutality, particularly those in which police have abused minorities. But there are other explanations for this behavior, both sociological and psychological. The explanation of prejudice does not require economic determinism. Gil's model seems like a forced explanation for the level of contemporary violence in America; it seems curiously dated, more suitable for an analysis of past cataclysms such as the French and Russian revolutions.

Economics, of course, plays a role in violence, both directly and indirectly. Statistics show that poverty is correlated with violent crime. Poor people are more likely to be arrested for violent criminal acts than middle class and well-to-do people. Rates of violent crime are highest among young people who are members of some ethnic and minority groups. There are undoubtedly Jean Valjean–like incidents of poor, hungry people stealing regularly for sustenance with violent interactions being a consequence somewhere along the line. Still one may question whether poverty tends to cause aggressive behavior directly or whether it is but a link in a complex chain of external events and psychological reactions. Writers who argue that poverty is neither a necessary nor sufficient condition for violence can point to numerous examples of people who were poor but not violent. A study of Chinese immigrants living in San Francisco showed that these immigrants had the highest unemployment rate in the city yet had remarkably low rates of violent crime.[65] An observation of C. Jencks puts the case succinctly, "If low income alone drove people to crime, graduate students and clergymen would also commit a lot of crimes."[66]

If poverty is not a necessary cause of the violence we see in the inner cities, how does poverty contribute to such behavior? A study by Nancy Guerra and her colleagues suggests that the association observed between poverty and aggression is partly attributable to the stresses that arise in low-income neighborhoods and the values tolerating aggressive acts that are part of the neighborhood culture. Guerra noted what we have already alluded to, that "Individuals living in inner-city communities are exposed to a relentless succession of stressful events in the context of chronically stressful conditions."[67] They go on further to state that "Poorer children are more likely to experience greater life events stress and neighborhood violence stress." In addition, "Poorer children are also more likely to adopt beliefs accepting of aggression. These beliefs and stresses predict early aggression that, in turn, predicts aggression in subsequent years."[68]

These ideas offer the beginning of an explanation. However,

continuing stress and cultural values that condone if not extol aggressive acts seem like only two pieces in a jigsaw puzzle in which there are still more to be found in the box. Other pieces in the puzzle may lie in the social structure of these communities. Wandersman and Nation suggested one of the pathways in which depressed structural characteristics in a neighborhood could promote crime and violence; when neighborhoods are economically impoverished, lack resources and witness a high turnover of population, it becomes difficult to maintain stable relationships.[69] Residents are less able to work together in informal ways and in establishing community organizations. The absence of such adult networks allows children to grow up without effective levels of social control. In depressed communities, the lack of external controls in the neighborhood compounds an all-too-prevalent tendency for families to be headed by uneducated single mothers with several children. Supervision and discipline of children may be sporadic. Without strongly developed internal controls, the child's standard of behavior may by default become those of the peer group, which can put the child on a collision course with the larger society. Early on, the children learn the survival skills taught in the streets, rather than the work ethic drummed into middle class children. Serious efforts to progress in school may be met with derision by one's peers. Short term gratification, including very early sexual experience, is the choice often made rather than delaying gratification and long term planning. Rates of teenage pregnancy and dropping out of school are high. Undereducated and undertrained, the prospect for good jobs in our new information technology–based economy are meager.

If we were able to wave a magic wand and cure all of these social ills in our urban centers, reducing violence to a level comparable to the rest of the society, we would as a nation still have levels of violence that are high compared to most other industrialized nations. Is there something in our national character that promotes violence?

This is a very difficult question to approach. Some see a clue in the proliferation of guns in our country. The number of firearms owned by Americans far exceeds that of most other developed countries. An argument promulgated by the gun lobby is that these weapons are necessary for protection of the home. However, statistics indicate that guns are much more likely to be used in domestic homicides than against robbers and thugs. A study carried out in the state of Washington found that guns kept at home resulted in the deaths of household members 18 times more often than in the deaths of strangers.[70]

Attempts to restrict the sale of guns in any way have been met with fervent resistance by the National Rifle Association. In listening to some gun owners argue on radio talk shows against gun control, one hears both passion and defiance. One wonders, how many people have an emotional investment in possessing this weapon of deadly force? Is it only a few like the callers on the talk shows, or are the numbers sizeable? Judging from the millions of guns owned by Americans, America's love affair with guns seems second only to its love affair with cars. Why? Is there something in our value systems that has placed guns in such a prized position?

Historically, our culture has emphasized individual initiative and self-reliance. In this context, self-protection was a logical extension of self-reliance. Guns were equalizers, mitigating disparities of physical strength. The prototype of a man's reliance on a gun was life as portrayed to us in the Old West where gunfights such as the shoot-out at the OK Corral became part of American folklore. Murder rates were particularly high in the frontier mining towns. Writing on violence in America, David T. Courtwright noted that the homicide rate of Nevada County, California, which included such mining camps as Guntown and Gemorrah, was on the order of 83 per 100,000 in the early 1850s.[71] Comparable rates in Boston and Philadelphia in the 1860s were of the order of six per 100,000. Courtwright described some of these small frontier communities (e.g., Julesburg and Laramie) as "murder-a-day railroad boomtowns."[72] Courtwright attributed these homicide rates in large part to the large gatherings of young men without the social control afforded by the presence of wives and family. The peer culture that developed put a premium on drinking, gambling, sensitivity about honor and carrying guns.

How much of the Wild West mentality persists to this day is a matter of conjecture. Interestingly, the gun-toting youth of our inner cities share a similarity with the gunfighters of the Western frontier in that many inner city youth do not see traditional law enforcement as a source of protection. Rather, they view the police more as harassers than protectors and feel that they must carry arms for self-defense. Students often report that the reason they bring weapons to the schoolroom is for self-protection to and from school. Along these lines, a 1998 report on safety in American schools estimated that there were more than 11,000 incidents of physical attacks or fights in which a weapon was used, and the problem was most prevalent in large schools.[73]

Parenthetically, some members of the mostly white militia movement in the United States take what appears to be an even more extreme position than the gun-carrying students. They believe that the government itself is the enemy and they must be prepared to fight the government.

The American public seems to tolerate a seemingly endless series of grizzly episodes such as a student in Kentucky firing guns into a school, killing children in a prayer circle. We wonder and lament, then shrug these things off and wait for the next incident. We buy home protection systems and build more prisons. The questions that really need to be addressed are: Are there effective ways of preventing such violence from occurring in the first place? And, if so, are we willing to commit the human and financial resources necessary to make a difference?

CHAPTER 4

Learning to Be Aggressive

C hildren learn much of their behavior patterns from modeling the behaviors of others they see around them. The way people behave in the home and in the neighborhood provides the early frames of reference for children as to what constitutes acceptable conduct. If the child witnesses frequent displays of verbal and physical aggression in the home, he or she is likely to view this behavior as natural, if not normative.

An egregious example of a violence-prone environment was described by James Garbarino in his book *Raising Children in a Socially Toxic Environment*. Mary, now a teenager, had been raised in a neighborhood in which she had been abused physically by her mother, beaten up on the street on several occasions and had been raped. Five members of her extended family had been killed in her young lifetime. Mary grew up learning that violence was part of the fabric of life in her community. As a teenager, she was accused of killing a girl with a gun while trying to steal her jacket. The shooting "came as the culmination of a string of incidents characterized by escalating violence."[1]

Children's beliefs about how acceptable it is to be aggressive seem rather fluid as they enter elementary school, and it takes a few years before their beliefs become crystallized. A study by L. Rowell Huesmann and Nancy Guerra found that children in a high-risk urban environment become much more accepting of aggression between the first and second grades.[2] Something about their early school culture promoted the value of being aggressive. Huesmann and Guerra observed that in the tough urban environments where these children lived, learning about aggression was a survival skill.

The Intergenerational Transmission of Aggression

What is the effect on a child of witnessing angry words exchanged by his or her parents, or worse, the father physically abusing the mother? The answers to these questions are complex. What we do know is that witnessing angry exchanges between parents causes distress in the child. Children exposed to even simulated anger between adults are likely to show physiological reactions (increased blood pressure and electrodermal reactivity) and report distress.[3] Children exposed to repeated marital discord have an increased risk of developing behavioral problems.

Imagine a child who witnesses episodes of domestic violence, his father striking, even injuring his mother. The child may want to intervene, yet is powerless to do so. Reactions of anger, anxiety and despair are all possible. How these emotions will play out in the child's development and later life is uncertain, but the insecurity produced in the child is not likely to have healthy consequences. Modeling theory suggests that the child is at risk for becoming aggressive.

A simplified view of modeling goes something like this: The child sees aggressive behavior that is essentially unpunished and seems to benefit the aggressor. He tries being aggressive himself, and finds that it brings more gain than pain, then consequently introduces it into his repertoire of behaviors. In applying this kind of paradigm to the unsettled emotions of a child after witnessing anger or violence between his parents, it seems reasonable that a child might be more likely to model this aggressiveness if at the same time he or she has had minimal development of the tender feelings of sympathy and empathy. If the child becomes hardened, the modeling of parental aggressiveness seems more likely.

Modeling of parental anger may be delayed or displaced onto other targets. Writing in the *Psychological Bulletin*, John Grych and Frank Fincham observed that modeling involves more than mimicking of behavior. "Modeling involves the acquisition of information about behavior. If parents are hostile and aggressive during conflicts, children may learn that aggression is an acceptable way to deal with disagreements. However, this belief is likely to be expressed in age-appropriate ways. Children who learn to be aggressive in conflictual situations might not aggress against their larger and more powerful parents, but may instead act aggressively when interacting with peers or younger children."[4] Grych and Fincham cite research in which children were exposed to angry interactions between adults. In their subsequent behavior toward playmates, the children increased their aggressiveness.

There is compelling evidence for the intergenerational transmission of aggression when the child is a direct victim of aggressive acts rather than a passive onlooker. Aggressive acts against the child may take the form of unusually severe discipline or may cross the line and become flagrant child abuse. In reviewing the research literature, Karlen Lyons-Ruth observed that "One of the best documented findings in the area of child psychopathology is the consistent relation between harsh and ineffective parental discipline and aggressive behavior problems."[5]

In working with angry and abusive people, therapists frequently find that their clients themselves had been abused as children. In studying the intergenerational transmission of aggression, researchers have often used the retrospective reports of adult abusers about what things were like in their homes when they were children. While such reports are not always reliable, the findings generally indicate that there is a greater chance of parents abusing their own children if the parents were themselves abused as children. It should be stressed, however, that most children who are abused do not become abusers. It is by no means an inevitability.

An example of a study showing the relation of excessive punishment and aggressiveness in boys was reported by Joana Haapasalo and Richard Tremblay.[6] School teachers rated their kindergarten pupils for overt physical aggressive behavior (e.g., fighting with other children, kicking, biting, bullying). The researchers found that the boys who continued to show aggressive patterns over a period of years were more likely to report that their parents used higher levels of punishment in disciplining them (e.g., slapping and hitting them, placing restrictions on them, calling them names) than children identified by their teachers as non-fighters. The chronically aggressive boys also reported less supervision by their parents than was the case for the non-fighting boys.

The assessments of parental discipline and supervision in the study were retrospective. In making these judgments one has to rely on the ability of the subjects to reconstruct events, which can be biased. Recently, however, a prospective study was reported in which assessments of parental discipline practices were made for several hundred preschool children in the late 1970s and early 1980s. In the 1990s when the children were adolescents, they were interviewed about assaultive behaviors such as being in gang fights, striking parents and using strong-arm methods to get money from other people. The researchers, Roy Herrenkohl and his colleagues, reported that the "more severe the physical discipline at preschool age, the higher the average level of physical assault in late adolescence."[7] The effects of early physical mistreatment of children can extend across a span of many years, influencing adolescent assaultive behavior.

When we think of adults physically abusing children, we usually think of adult members of the child's family—typically the father or mother. However, it wasn't that long ago when physical abuse of children was also institutionalized in some schools. Teachers had the prerogative of flogging their students for disciplinary problems. In his autobiography, Winston Churchill related how in the boys' school he first attended, the boys were assembled in the library, and in the adjoining room, two or three misbehaving boys would be flogged with birch until they bled. Churchill noted that the assembled students would quake while listening to the screams of their fellow students.[8] This exercise was supposed to improve character.

Long Term Effects of Child Abuse

The study by Herrenkohl and his colleagues suggests that physical abuse of children is a risk factor for violence in adolescence. Indeed, researchers have found that adolescents who are aggressive and violent are more likely to have experienced physical abuse during childhood than comparison groups. Studies, for example, of violent adolescents living in residential facilities have found that these young people have experienced higher rates of physical abuse than less violent and non-violent comparison groups.[9] High school students who have been violent with their dates were more likely to have experienced physical abuse than non-violent students.[10]

Parental aggression against the child may have a very long reach. In a prospective study in which boys were followed for 30 years, a relation was found between parental aggression and the individual's subsequent involvement in personal crimes such as murder, rape and assault.[11]

A graphic example of the long range effects of physical abuse of the child is the case of Ricky, described in Garbarino's book. Ricky, now a teenager, "described in detail the physical violence he had experienced and learned at home—a father who assaulted him regularly with his fists, beat him once with a two-by-four, and another time slammed his head against a pool table."[12] Now, Ricky faced a life sentence for killing one of his friends with a stolen pistol while under the influence of drugs.

A Few Hours in the Lives of Abusive Parents

Women were selected from the case files of the New York State Department of Social Services for study. The women were included in the study if their records indicated that there was physical evidence that they had physically abused one of their children, such as leaving welts or bruises on the child that persisted for 48 hours after the incident was reported. Observers went into the women's homes for three consecutive days and for a period of 90 minutes on each day recorded observations of the mother and their children. These observations were compared with those made on a control group of mothers who had no record of child abuse. The researchers reported that the mothers in the control group were much more likely to interact with their children, to play with them, to hug or caress them, to praise and compliment them and to instruct them. In contrast, the abusive mothers were much more likely to yell or scream at their children and to slap or hit them. The differences in parent-child interactions between the groups of mothers were pronounced.[13]

How did the children behave during the observational periods? The children in the homes of the abusive mothers were more verbally and physically aggressive than the children in the homes of the control group. David Bousha and Craig Twentyman, who carried out the study, noted that "These data are consistent with a social learning concept of aggression that emphasizes the role of maternal modeling in children's violent behavior."[14]

Both unresponsive parenting and excessive harsh discipline have been linked to aggressiveness in children. So too is the simple lack of two parents in the home. Studies have shown that the children of single mothers are more likely to engage in aggressive behavior than children who live in two-parent homes.[15] Lack of supervision probably plays a role here. There may be no one around to put a lid on the child's aggressive acts. Research carried out by a team led by Janis Kupersmidt found that the relation between single parent households and childhood aggressiveness seemed most pronounced in low-income families.[16] Middle class families seem better able to compensate for the absence of a parent.

Aggressiveness in Toddlers

How early in life do aggressive tendencies show themselves? Research suggests that the answer is very early. Daniel Shaw and his colleagues at the University of Pittsburgh were able to document clear differences in aggressive behaviors in children who were between one and two years old.[17] They set up an experimental situation in which the child spent some of the time with his or her mother and some of the time separated from her. At times toys were available for the child to play with and at times the child had no toys. The sessions, lasting about two hours, were videotaped through a one-way mirror. The children in the study were observed at age 12 months, 18 months and 24 months. The observers looked for evidence of aggressive reactions (e.g., throwing toys at the mother or examiner; hitting, biting or kicking the mother or examiner; hammering the mirror in the room; pounding or stepping on the toys; and kicking the door). The researchers found that at the 18-month observational period, some children were peaceful while others were aggressive, and some were judged severely aggressive.

The study carried out by Shaw and his colleagues provided a nice demonstration that the behavior of the mother toward the child has an impact on the child's aggressiveness. While observing the mother and the child in the experimental situation, the research team was able to make assessments of the mother's responsiveness to the child. The researchers found that when mothers were judged less responsive to their infants at age 12 months, the children tended to be more aggressive when subsequently observed at age 24 months.[18] Interestingly, this relation held for infant boys but not for infant girls.

The Mind Set of Aggressive Youth

Experiments conducted by psychologists suggest that aggressive adolescents and young adults have a mind set to see hostile intent in the actions of other people. They may not only be quick to interpret the behavior of others as hostile when it was not so intended, they may also be prone to interpret facial expressions and body language as signaling hostile intent. A glaring example is the incident where a biker struck by an automobile charged the driver and shot her in the head. The biker acted as if he were under attack and was reported to have said as much. How many times have we heard about young people resorting to violence after saying they were "disrespected?" The alleged disrespect might have been an innocuous expression on someone's face.

Here are some representative experiments that demonstrate a tendency for aggressive youth to read negative intent in the appearance of other people. William Nasby and his colleagues studied 40 emotionally disturbed boys in a residential treatment facility. The boys were first assessed on a measure of "unsocialized aggression," which included such items as "fighting, impertinence, use of profanity, and temper tantrums."[19] The boys were then shown 20 different facial photographs of a woman who had been asked to portray various emotions. Each of the boys was asked to sort the facial photographs into groups "that he thought expressed the same (or a similar) emotion or feeling."[20] The examiner then asked the boys to describe the basis on which they had sorted the photographs. The researchers recorded the terms the boys used in describing the groups of photographs. The researchers found that the more aggressive boys were more likely than the less aggressive boys to use words suggesting hostility or aggressiveness when describing the facial expressions of these photographs.

Kenneth Dodge and his colleagues carried out a study using 128 adolescent boys in a maximum security prison for juvenile offenders.[21] They showed the boys video tapes that portrayed two adolescents interacting, with one boy experiencing a negative outcome (e.g., at school, one boy damages the other boy's metal shop project). The inmates were asked to imagine that they were the person in the scene who experienced the negative outcome. After viewing each video tape, the boys were asked to use a multiple choice format to describe the other boy's intent. The four choices were: (1) it was to be mean; (2) it was an accident; (3) it was to be helpful; and (4) it was unclear why he did it. The researchers reported that the more times the boys had been arrested for violent crimes, the more likely they were to attribute mean intent to the boy portrayed in the video vignettes.

Rush to Judgment

In the incident in which the bicyclist killed the driver of the car that had struck him, it was clear that he made a rapid decision. The circumstances of the accident seemed evidence enough of the other party's hostile intent and he responded with violence almost instantly. A rush to judgment may be another characteristic of aggressive boys.

An interesting experiment, again carried out by Kenneth Dodge with Joseph Newman, documented this tendency in elementary school boys.[22] The boys were told they were going to play a detective game. They listened to stories describing a hostile act, for example, an incident in which an elderly woman called the school, complaining that a student had deliberately spilled her groceries and run away. The woman said that she thought she knew the name of the boy but wasn't sure. After one of the children in the study heard the story, he was told that he could listen to up to five taped testimonies by different peers of the suspect to help him decide whether the individual had committed the act. The boys were told that they could listen to as many of the five tapes as they wanted to in order to reach their decision. The tapes contained some sentences that implicated the suspect ("I saw him running in the direction of that woman's house yesterday after school.") and some sentences that were ambiguous or exculpatory.[23]

Aggressive boys were picked out by their teachers and their

classmates. Their responses to the detective game were compared with the responses of children who were judged to be nonaggressive. The aggressive boys chose to hear 30 percent fewer testimonies before making their decisions than did the nonaggressive boys.

Interestingly, there appears to be a similar mind set in adult men who are prone to marital violence. Christopher Eckhardt and his colleagues asked men with a history of violence against their wives to listen to several tape-recorded dramas performed by professional actors.[24] The dramas (e.g., the man overhears a conversation between his wife and her friend, saying unpleasant things about the man) were calculated to arouse feelings of anger and jealousy. The subjects in the study were asked to imagine that they were involved in the situation and to express their own thoughts and feelings into a tape recorder. Their comments were compared with those from married men who had not been violent with their wives. The thought patterns of the violence-prone men were more likely to magnify the importance of these negative events, to look at the situation in stark black and white terms, to make arbitrary inferences about the other person's behavior in the absence of confirming evidence and to show little control over anger. As was the case in the research on aggressive children, there was a tendency to see the worst, to rush to judgment and to act precipitously.

Seeing hostile threats in others and rushing to judgment can lead to acts with lethal outcomes. The case of the biker in Maryland who shot the motorist is an example. Another widely publicized incident occurred in Baton Rouge, Louisiana. A 16-year-old Japanese exchange student knocked on the door of a suburban house asking for directions. The owner of the house, believing he was being threatened, called out to the student, warning him. The student did not comprehend what the man was saying. The man reacted by shooting and killing the student.[25]

The tendency to react rapidly without giving a matter adequate consideration seems to be associated with starting fights in children. Jeffrey Halperin and his colleagues studied children (ages 7–13) who had been referred to an urban outpatient child psychiatry clinic.[26] Children who had a history of initiating physical fights were compared with children who didn't fight, on an experimental test of impulsivity that involved the task of identifying letters presented in very brief time exposures (a fraction of a second). An impulsive response was considered to be a judgment initiated prior to the time that all the necessary information was available. The researchers reported that children with a history of starting fights made more impulsivity errors than those who did not initiate fights.

Another aspect of mind set that may differentiate aggressive and non-aggressive children is what psychologists call "locus of control of reinforcement." The concept deals with the degree to which an individual believes he or she is able to bring about the things he or she wants to attain in life and how much he or she feels those things are out of his or her control. The internally-oriented view is, "I am the master of my fate. My actions will make a difference." The externally-oriented view is, "I'm being buffeted around and there's not much I can do about it." Call your adversary "fate," "the will of the gods" or the "machinations of some giant corporations," the external view is that your own efforts are not likely to matter.

Studies carried out by Thomas Ollendick and his colleagues suggest that aggressive youth tend to view the outcomes of their interactions as externally rather than internally controlled. In commenting on their findings, the researchers observed that aggressive youths felt that they had little control or influence over what happened to them, and that even if they did perform well, the desired social outcomes wouldn't follow.[27] The inference from these studies is that many aggressive boys may not see a realistic possibility of taking control over their lives—at least through the traditional channels of opportunity that society provides. Aggressiveness may be a crude, at times, effective way of coping under these circumstances—of both gaining something material from the society and of lashing out at others in reaction to feelings of perpetual frustration.

The Continuity of Aggressive Behavior Over the Years

Children who are aggressive in their early school years are at risk for developing psychological problems and of engaging in anti-social and delinquent behaviors. Early aggressive behaviors are likely to bring on rejection by other children. By the early elementary grades, many children take a dim view of their aggressive peers. They see aggressive children as responsible for their actions and feel angry and unsympathetic toward them. Children who strike other children without provocation and are argumentative and disruptive in the classroom tend to have few friends. The combination of aggressiveness and peer rejection often leads to a troubled youngster. In following children who were evaluated as aggressive and rejected in the third grade, John Coie and his colleagues at Duke University reported that "Children who were both rejected and aggressive in third grade were more than three times as likely to have poor adjustment at the end of the first year of middle school as those children who were neither aggressive nor rejected."[28]

There is a fairly high chance that children who are identified as aggressive at an early age will continue to be aggressive when assessed in later years. Studies of the stability of aggression over time indicate that many children who are aggressive as young children continue to be aggressive as they grow older. In a study carried out in Canada, children's aggressiveness was assessed at three-year intervals. The research team led by D.S. Moskowitz reported that aggression was a moderately stable characteristic for both boys and girls over the three-year time periods.[29]

Aggressive children are more likely to become delinquent as adolescents. Judith Brook and her colleagues followed elementary school age children well into adolescence and found that childhood aggression was a precursor of teenage delinquency.[30] In a study carried out in Sweden, Hakan Stattin and David Magnusson followed more than 1,000 children from the third grade to adulthood.[31] Aggressiveness in the primary schools was measured by teacher ratings. Delinquency was defined as registered lawbreaking and was assessed until age 27. The researchers reported that for boys there was a strong connection between the aggressiveness ratings made by the teachers in childhood and subsequent adult delinquency. They found that high rates of aggression were characteristic of boys who later committed violent crimes.

In a review article, Rolf Loeber and Thomas Dishion pointed out that "Aggressiveness from adolescence onward is a more or less continuous predictor of delinquency."[32] It almost looks as if the transition from aggression in childhood to adult criminality is a prophesy unfolding.

However, a closer look at the statistics indicates that there is no inevitability in the progression of childhood aggression into adult criminality. In reviewing these studies, Julie O'Donnell and her colleagues noted that "Over half of boys who are aggressive in childhood avoid continuing involvement in aggression or escalation to other problem behaviors."[33] In commenting on their own findings, Stattin and Magnusson observed that "Even though the relation between early aggressiveness and later crime was quite substantial, the high percentage of false positives and false negatives makes it hazardous to predict crime on an individual basis."[34]

So we have a situation in which roughly half of the children picked out as aggressive in early school years will get into trouble later while the other half will not. What is it that makes the difference? Research reported by O'Donnell and her colleagues sheds some light on the question. They followed 10- and 11-year-old boys picked out by their teachers as aggressive to see which of the boys would become involved in delinquency or substance abuse during the next three years. The researchers found that the level of the child's earlier aggressiveness was not a good predictor of later problems. Once aggressiveness was noticeable enough for his teacher to readily identify him as "aggressive," that was all that was necessary to indicate that the child was at risk for further trouble. If a child's level of aggressiveness went beyond that point, it added little to the ability to predict subsequent delinquency. What is a better predictor of future trouble for these 10- to 11-year-old aggressive boys is the company they keep. O'Donnell's team observed that "Interaction with antisocial peers was consistently predictive of involvement in delinquency and substance use among these aggressive boys."[35] One might offer a formula that early aggressiveness plus associating with bad company augurs future trouble.

Externalizing Behavior

Children's aggressive behavior often occurs as part of a larger pattern of behavior that has been called externalizing behavior. Not only are such children aggressive, they may be defiant, impulsive, disruptive and overactive. Contrast this behavior with what has been called internalizing behavior, where children appear withdrawn, anxious and depressed. Neither pattern is desirable; both merit the concern of parents and possible therapeutic intervention.

Externalizing behavior, which is our focus here, often leads to social consequences such as peer rejection and has consequences for intellectual development as well. Externalizing behavior can be distinguished into two types: one pattern involves inattention and hyperactivity, the other, aggressive-conduct problems characterized by violence and rule-breaking. In the early school years, hyperactivity is often associated with underachievement in school, particularly difficulties in learning to read. Aggressive behavior by itself in the earlier years is not likely to have a dramatic effect on reading levels but when combined with hyperactivity, the effect can be substantial. It was reported that children who are both hyperactive and aggressive were five times as likely not to show the expected progress in reading as other children.[36]

Researchers have reported an inverse association between measures of children's I.Q. and their level of aggressiveness. Two types of explanations were advanced for this observed relation. The first explanation held that a lower I.Q. made achievement in school difficult, leaving the child frustrated. Aggressiveness was a reaction to this frustration. It is a scenario of lashing out where the child sees success for others but not for himself or herself. The second line of explanation is that an aggressive child simply doesn't fit into and work well in a structured learning environment and is not able to fully develop the verbal and computational skills that are important for academic progress.

When children are followed over many years into adulthood, it looks as if measures of early aggressiveness are more predictive of later (adult) I.Q. scores than the other way around. L. Rowell Huesmann and his colleagues noted that the results of their long-term study "suggest that aggression interferes with the development of intellectual functioning."[37] They observed, "Although diminished intellectual abilities and academic failure may well stimulate aggressive responses in the young child, whatever effect intelligence has on aggressive behavior, it appears to have occurred by age 8.... These data do demonstrate, however, that regardless of a young child's I.Q., intellectual achievements, both currently and up to middle adulthood, are adversely affected by aggressive behavior." The intellectually competent adults in the study had childhoods characterized by identification with the parents, lower levels of aggressive behavior, and less rejection, restriction and punishment by the parents.

Making Boys into Soldiers

Sometimes boys become violent not from happenstance, but from deliberate training. In lands as disparate as Burma, Sudan, Sri Lanka, Chechnya, Liberia, Angola and the West Bank of the Jordan, young children have been recruited as soldiers. *Images Asia*, a non-governmental agency based in Thailand, reported that the Burmese army recruited child soldiers from street children, orphans and refugees. While the children were given menial jobs such as cooking or carrying ammunition, they also served in combat, sometimes in human-wave assaults.[38]

Chicago Tribune writer Liz Sly related the story of Roland Sengbeh, who at the age of 16 was a veteran of Liberia's Civil War.[39] He was a captain in a Small Boy Unit in one of Liberia's armed factions, and was in command of 52 children. He owned his own AK-47 automatic weapon, firing it in combat. For four years he had fought in Liberia and had taken a bullet in his leg. Observers have reported that many of the children seemed to enjoy their life as soldiers, talking about it like an adventure. They have raped, killed and looted.

Training young boys into killing machines can take various forms. In *Paris-Match*, Jacques-Maria Bourget described the training of Palestinian youngsters to become terrorists.[40] The children were told that if they died they would sit at the right hand side of Allah. One technique that was used to harden recruits was to have them sleep in specially dug graves. Some recruits were buried alive to provide them with near-death experiences.

Caroline Moorehead described the indoctrination of a young boy into soldiering in the wars in Sudan.[41] The boy started his military life at age 11. The weapon he carried was larger than he was. His first order, a task to prove that he "was worthy," was to execute a prisoner. When he protested, he was told he would be killed himself if he refused. He shot the prisoner. In subsequent months, he witnessed gang rapes, and he himself pushed people into wells and left them to die. He belonged to a tough outfit. As a form of punishment, his elbows were often tied together tightly behind his back, hurting his ribs. To make him brave in battle, he was given amphetamines.

The desensitization to killing that was part of the learning experience of the young Sudanese soldier has parallels in earlier conflicts.

In the Japanese conquest of China before and during World War II, some Japanese soldiers were ordered to bayonet Chinese prisoners. Iris Chang described how a Japanese lieutenant ordered his troops to engage in some "killing practice."[42] He explained that the Chinese should not be considered human beings, but had less value than dogs or cats. When none of the troops volunteered for this human bayonet practice, he became incensed, called the men cowards and then ordered them to do it, calling out the names of individual soldiers, one by one. One of the soldiers reported how he shut his eyes, bayonetted the helpless prisoner, and thought himself a murderer as he did it.

Writing in the *Bulletin of the Atomic Scientists*, psychologist Mike Wessells noted that the recruitment of boys into military and paramilitary units is sometimes voluntary and sometimes forced.[43] In some countries where there has been longstanding ethnic and religious conflict, peer pressure—boys urging other boys to join the unit—is a factor in recruitment. Sometimes boys join these military organizations for adventure. In past centuries, boys served as midshipmen in the British Navy. However, many boys today are forced into military units. Wessells reported that militias have abducted children at gunpoint. In some countries—Afghanistan, Bhutan, Burma, Ethiopia, Mozambique and El Salvador—soldiers have taken children from schools. A Burmese recruit related how government soldiers surrounded his school and arrested 40 to 50 youth while the teachers fled in fear. In Ethiopia, armed militias surrounded marketplaces ordering every male who appeared eligible into a truck.

Is there any hope for the boys—recruited as children, trained to accept violence and become violent themselves—to return to their communities and live normal, productive lives? After observing some of these children in a rehabilitation camp in Sierra Leone, Wessells expressed some optimism. He saw evidence that the boys' behavior could be turned in a positive directions—to games rather than war. In some cultures, traditional healing ceremonies have helped engineer this transition. In one African village, a traditional healer spoke of a ritual he used to purify former boy soldiers. Initially, he lived with the child for a month, during which time he fed him a special diet designed to cleanse the child. After the month had passed, the healer convened the village for a ceremony. In the ceremony, the healer buried weapons—machetes and rifles. Then he announced that as of this day, the boy's life as a soldier was over and his life as a citizen had begun.

Turning Women into Warriors

While many studies show that women tend to be less aggressive than men, there is little doubt that women can be trained to be very aggressive. One of the most flagrant examples is the report of girl soldiers on the island of Sri Lanka. Writing in the Swedish magazine *Amnesty Press*, Martin Adler reported that the separatist movement in Sri Lanka has recruited girls since the 1980s.[44] After a period of harsh physical and mental training, the girls were issued cyanide tablets to carry around their necks with instructions to kill themselves if captured. The girls were said to be skilled in combat and to be more fanatical than their male counterparts.

Reporter Dana Priest described the aggressiveness and macho behaviors of some American women soldiers serving as military police in Bosnia.[45] One soldier became so excited in the mess hall that she spread her feet apart, reached for an imaginary weapon and in pantomime sprayed the wall with bullets. Later she related that she loved firing the grenade launcher that is mounted on top of the armored vehicle she rides in. She talked of firing a Serb AK-47 automatic rifle on a practice range and letting out a guttural yell. When interviewed, the commander of the brigade observed that it was important to instill a warrior spirit in the women soldiers. She said that if the women thought like warriors, believed they were warriors, then they would do what was needed. The commander reflected that most women wouldn't feel they have it in them, but once that warrior spirit was unleashed, you'd find that aggressiveness.

Teaching Men to Be Torturers

There are still dictators in the world community, men who can imprison their opponents without cause, torture them, even execute them. But these dictators seem to be a dwindling species. In the years following World War II until the end of the cold war, there were many more of these individuals in power.

It wasn't that long ago, in the late 1960s and early 1970s, that even the cradle of democracy—Greece—was ruled by a military government. During this period, the government sanctioned the torture of political prisoners. The individuals chosen to carry out such torture were members of a special unit, the ESA (Army Police Corps). We have learned much about the way the members of this special unit were selected and trained, thanks to in-depth interviews carried out with ex-members of the unit. The story was reported in a 1986 article in *Psychology Today* by Janice Gibson and Mika Haritos-Fatouros.[46]

Initial screening for membership in the unit was based on physical strength and appropriate political beliefs. The idea was to recruit people who had absorbed in their childhood and adolescence hostile attitudes toward the people they would be torturing. The training process had the objective of making the men selected absolutely obedient to their officers, to do whatever was asked. Training began with brutal initiation rites; the recruits were punched, kicked and flogged. An esprit de corps was cultivated by repeated declarations of how important and special this unit was. A special language was created for members to describe themselves and their victims. Prisoners were often referred to as worms that had to be crushed.

Sensitivity to meting out torture was systematically diminished during training. The recruits were first forced to endure torture themselves. Then, those chosen to inflict torture were brought to the prison where they stood on guard watching veterans in the unit torture the prisoners. Next, they were required to participate in group beatings of the prisoners. Finally, they were instructed to apply a variety of torture methods to the prisoners. This step-by-step procedure eased them into the role of torturers.

If the men in the unit ever developed remorse about what they were doing and tried to help the prisoners, they knew that they would be treated like the prisoners themselves. The men also believed that they were being spied upon regularly by fellow soldiers, which further acted to keep them in line.

Raising Less Aggressive Children

Looking at the other side of the coin, let's ask the question, what kind of parenting behavior is likely to engender less aggressiveness in children and fewer conduct problems? A review of more than 40 studies carried out by Fred Rothbaum and John Weisz suggests that parenting approaches that emphasize positive reactions to children (approval, acceptance, responsiveness, support), that avoid coercive control, and in which parents attempt to tune into the child's world and offer appropriate guidance, are most likely to lead to this kind of outcome.[47] It is a picture of being alert to the child's thoughts and needs, guiding as needed and emphasizing positive rather than negative feedback to the child.

In his review of studies of peaceful societies, Bonta offered some observations about child-rearing practices that are interesting, though not necessarily translatable into a society like ours. Bonta reported that in some of these societies, very young children experienced a precipitous drop in the attention adults and children paid to them. There was a "dramatic plunge in status of 2-to-3-year-olds."[48] From birth until this age the infant was fondled repeatedly and nursed on demand. Their needs were quickly satisfied. Then suddenly everything changed. From being the center of attention, the child now received hardly any attention. The child's tantrums and protests were ignored by everyone. No one paid any attention. The child was made to feel like he or she was an insignificant member of the community. The influential psychiatrist Alfred Adler once talked about the reactions of the first born child to the attention now offered to his newborn sibling as that of a "dethroned monarch."[49] What happens to the youngsters in these peaceful societies may be similar.

Another observation of Bonta's may offer more possibilities for application in our society, namely—peaceful, cooperative attitudes can be taught. As an example, consider the Hutterite communities. Children are taught cooperative values in the home and the values are reinforced in the community. The children are so well taught that by the time they attend public school, teachers find it difficult to motivate the children using competitive strategies.[50]

Finally, Bonta's observations suggest that children's games provide another opportunity for non-aggressive societies to promote cooperative rather than competitive values. American games and sports are often quite competitive. Sports teach the child about winning and losing and as such serve as useful preparation for living in a competitive, market-driven society. In the nonaggressive societies

Bonta reviewed, children play in a way that minimizes competition. They play games involving hiding, catching or spinning tops, but the stress is on having fun, not winning or losing. This is light years' distance from an American football coach's observation that losing was like death.

CHAPTER 5

Anger, Aggression and the Individual

N early everyone feels angry at times. For most of us, the feeling of anger does not inevitably lead to an aggressive act. For some people, anger rarely if ever finds its way into an injurious act. But for others, aggressive acts are not uncommon. And if aggressive acts occur and occur frequently, what consequences do they entail? Are the effects likely to be positive for the individual, negative—or possibly both?

And what about anger itself? Could feeling angry have any positive value for the individual in his or her daily life, or does anger essentially have negative effects on the individual's health and well being?

These are provocative questions for which we will have to grope for answers. In an essay on anger, Raymond Novaco observed that "Anger is a normal emotion that has considerable adaptive value for coping with the adversities of a depersonalized social world and can facilitate perseverance in the face of frustration or injustice. Because anger can mobilize our psychological resources and can energize behaviors that take corrective action, we need a capacity for anger as a survival mechanism."[1]

Novaco's words have the ring of believability if we let our minds search through the pages of history. It must have been a pretty angry lot of colonials who carried out the Boston Tea Party and set the

85

stage for the American Revolution. The same could be said for the citizens of Paris who stormed the Bastille, an act of great significance in the French Revolution. Anger can both stiffen the resolve needed to prevail in a long-term conflict and be an impetus for taking immediate actions, including high-risk actions. We mentioned how some football coaches try to stir up anger in their players in the hopes of improving their performance on the field. But as some athletes have suggested, while playing angry may lead to playing harder, it could also lead to playing dumber. Indeed, acting while angry has led to innumerable incidents of mayhem and murder. "Cooling off" can be a life-saver.

It is difficult to focus on the positive effects of anger without touching on the negative ones. Although anger can be a motivator, it is often an explosive and volatile one. Clearly, anger can produce unfortunate as well as desirable consequences. We might begin our consideration of the downside of anger by posing a set of questions. Think back to the last time you felt really angry. Recall the circumstances. Now think about how you felt. Was it a comfortable experience or an uncomfortable experience? How was your concentration affected? How well were you able to attend to the business of the day—focusing on what you were planning to do? Did you find your attention willy nilly drifting to the anger-arousing situation and the person or persons that triggered these angry feelings?

Anger and Physical Symptoms

The idea that psychological factors affect one's health is not a new idea, though it is currently receiving a lot of attention. Today, there is much discussion of mind-body relations. Contemporary interest in the problem received an impetus from the publication of Franz Alexander's book *Psychosomatic Medicine*.[2] In the book, Alexander postulated that there was a relation between personality characteristics such as hostility and dependency and certain chronic diseases. In addition to such personality characteristics, researchers and clinicians have pointed to the role of stress and depression in the formation of physical symptoms.

Some years ago, I wrote a monograph reviewing the research that bore on Alexander's formulations.[3] In regard to hostility, there was some evidence that it was associated with certain diseases. For example, consider the skin disorder neurodermatitis. Alexander viewed the act of scratching one's skin (which he felt contributed to the problem) was a displacement of hostile impulses from an original target—presumably another person—onto oneself. And indeed, some researchers found that people with neurodermatitis tended to have problems relating to hostility.

An early study carried out by M.E. Allerhand and his colleagues illustrated the point well. They used a self-report questionnaire to compare neurodermatitis patients with two control groups, patients with skin diseases of presumed non-psychogenic origin and general medical patients. The researchers found that the neurodermatitis patients more frequently showed impatience with others and felt irritable when experiencing minor frustrations. These patients were more likely to check such items as, "I must admit that I am a high-strung person"; "I must admit that it makes me angry when other people interfere with my daily activity"; and "At times I feel like smashing things."[4]

I worked with a neurodermatitis patient who presented a textbook case of what the research literature was suggesting. She was a late-middle-aged woman who lived alone in an apartment house. In many ways, she was dependent on her daughter, a busy single mother, for company. When her daughter had other things to do, my patient felt extremely neglected and aggrieved. In my patient's eyes, her daughter had not put her (the mother) sufficiently high on her priority list and this transgression was a constant irritant. My patient's resentment and her anger mounted. At the same time, her scratching increased and her skin condition worsened. When I suggested in therapy that she needed to examine her dependency on her daughter and to consider making changes in her life, she responded by calling her dermatologist and asking for more skin cream.

Arnold Meyerburg, Roland Tanck and I wondered whether anger had any relation to the garden variety physical symptoms (e.g. headaches, weakness, back problems, diarrhea) that people often experience. We gave out our structured diaries to 85 undergraduate students and asked them to fill them out at night for a period of one week. We found that the diary measure of interpersonal stress, which included items dealing with anger, was correlated with the number of physical symptoms the students reported. Interpersonal stress was particularly high on the days when these symptoms were reported.[5]

We repeated the study with another sample of university students and once again found that interpersonal stress was positively related to reports of symptoms.[6] The specific role of anger in the relation, however, was equivocal. In the first sample, both anger items (reports of feeling and expressing anger) were positively related to reports of physical symptoms, while in the second sample they were not.

In a further analysis of our diary data, we looked at the qualitative responses the students made to the questions, comparing the students who reported many physical symptoms with those who reported very few. We found that the students with many symptoms were much more preoccupied with interpersonal problems, usually involving peers. The students expressed feelings of unfulfilled expectations regarding the behavior of others accompanied by feelings of resentment. A typical response was, "I'm angry at my boyfriend—but more hurt than angry."[7] Our studies suggested that anger was involved in commonplace somatic reactions, but probably not in isolation. What was taking place seemed to be an experience of difficulties in relationships in which frustration, disappointment and anger were parts of the mix. When a person felt this complex of emotions, they seemed more prone to develop physical symptoms.

Elaine, a woman in her late 20s, provides a good example of a romantic quandary many people experience. She had been dating a man for some months and began to sleep over at his apartment. She wanted to marry him. One evening he told her he loved her, said he was going to write his family about her, and asked her to go away with him for the weekend. Hardly had he spoken these long sought after words when he began to backtrack. Soon, everything was put off, including the weekend trip. Elaine reacted with anger, storming out of his apartment. Later, she returned to retrieve her belongings. Her boyfriend's Hamlet act had raised her hopes, then dashed them. She felt hurt and angry, then became depressed.

Jenny, a woman in her late 20s, had a somewhat similar experience. She fell in love with a married man, who at the time had been separated from his wife for about four months. Then, he began to see his wife off and on. Finally, he reunited with his wife, leaving Jenny frustrated, angry and depressed. She wanted to be with him, but couldn't even telephone him. She waited for his calls that might or might not come. She felt upset, at times panicky, and both angry at him and herself for getting into this position.

Type A and Your Heart

Of all the diseases that may have links to hostility, the most attention has been given to coronary heart disease. In 1974, Meyer Friedman and Ray Rosenman published an influential book titled *Type A Behavior and Your Heart.*[8] The thesis of the book was that it was possible to describe people in terms of two personality types (labeled Type A and Type B) and that persons who were Type A were more prone to develop coronary heart disease. Type A was not conceived as a single characteristic; rather, it was viewed as a complex of characteristics. In a review of research on Type A and coronary heart disease, Stephanie Booth-Kewley and Howard Friedman offered a concise description of Type A behavior. Type A "refers broadly to the behavior pattern of any person who is involved in an aggressive and incessant struggle to achieve more and more in less and less time." Further, "Such personalities are characterized by competitive achievement striving, a sense of time urgency and impatience, aggressiveness, and easily aroused hostility."[9]

The idea that a pattern of behavior might have a significant impact on the development of coronary heart disease was something that gradually took shape in the minds of Friedman and Rosenman, both cardiologists working in a San Francisco medical center, and their associate, biochemist Sanford Byers. The three became suspicious that stress might be involved in heart disease. As a first tentative step in exploring this possibility, they sent out questionnaires to several hundred industrialists and physicians soliciting their opinions as to what had caused a heart attack in a friend or patient. They found that 70 percent of the businessmen and a similar number of physicians believed that stress associated with meeting deadlines and excessive competitive drive had been the major causes of the heart attack.[10] The researchers followed this exploratory study with sophisticated epidemiological and clinical studies that tended to confirm their hypothesis that Type A behavior pattern was linked to coronary heart disease.

In a more recent book, *Treating Type A Behavior and Your Heart*, Friedman and Diane Ulmer offered some additional thoughts about the concept of Type A. They wrote, "The Type A personality is dominated by covert insecurity of status or hyperaggressiveness, or both."[11] They further noted that "Type A behavior erupts most frequently in a person already aggressive and unsure about his status when he encounters situations that he construes as either status-threatening or irritating and anger-provoking. It is only then that the struggle ensues, bringing in its wake a sense of time urgency or free-floating hostility, and, after the passage of many years, the tendency to self-destruct."[12]

The authors viewed hyperaggressiveness as not simply a wish to achieve or compete successfully but a desire to dominate with little concern about the feelings or rights of one's competitors. The image that is evoked is of the business tycoon who crushes his opponents by means fair and foul. We have talked about the confluence of such acquisitive and power needs in the context of wars unleashed by nation states. Friedman and Ulmer's portrait of the hyperaggressive individual is conceptually similar to the analysis we presented of the motives underlying warfare. Indeed, some Type A people view everyday life as war.

Free-floating hostility was described by Friedman and Ulmer as "permanently dwelling anger that shows itself with ever greater frequency in response to increasingly trivial happenings."[13] This hostility, in part, is an outflow of thwarted hyperaggressiveness. The individual seems chronically irritable. His or her opinions are often cast in violent terms; the people involved may be castigated. The reaction to a mistake in a game of bridge or tennis may be explosive. Even conversation at the dinner table may be punctuated with hostility.

Researchers have evaluated individuals for Type A behavior by using two approaches, structured interviews and a questionnaire. In the interviews, people were asked about the usual way they responded to situations that might bring on competitiveness, impatience or hostility. The interview procedure allowed the researcher not only to evaluate the person's statements, but to make assessments of his or her speech characteristics—such as how rapidly the person talked, loudness and explosiveness. The questionnaire was a traditional self-report instrument that yielded a number of measures such as speed and impatience, job involvement, and hard-driving competitiveness.

Over the years, many studies have been carried out relating these measures to indicators of coronary heart disease. After examining the findings of studies using the statistical technique of meta-analysis, Booth-Kewley and Friedman drew the following conclusions.

1. Type A behavior is reliably related to coronary heart disease. The relation, however, is modest, not large.

2. The Structured Interview measure of Type A behavior is a better predictor of coronary heart disease than the questionnaire measure.

3. The hard-driving, competitive aspects of the Type A personality may have some influence on coronary heart disease, but simply being heavily involved in a job or working rapidly does not. Anger and hostility, however, seem to relate to coronary heart disease.[14]

Booth-Kewley and Friedman summarized their evaluation of this research as follows: "Overall, the picture of the coronary-prone personality emerging from this review does not appear to be that of the workaholic, hurried, impatient individual, which is probably the image most frequently associated with coronary proneness. Rather, the true picture seems to be one of a person with one or more negative emotions: perhaps someone who is depressed, aggressively competitive, easily frustrated, anxious, angry, or some combination."[15]

In their review Booth-Kewley and Friedman noted that anger, hostility and aggression all relate to coronary heart disease, with hostility showing the strongest association.

In a recent paper, Todd Miller and his colleagues confirmed the important role of hostility in coronary heart disease. They observed, "In recent years, hostility has emerged as the most important personality variable in psychosocial research on the etiology of CHD [coronary heart disease]."[16] This conclusion was based on the studies that Booth-Kewley and Friedman had reviewed plus 30 new independent studies. Again, using a meta-analysis, they concluded that hostility was an independent risk factor for coronary heart disease.

Type A behavior characteristics may also play a role, albeit probably not a large one, in elevated blood pressure in some people. The evidence indicates that in response to stress, Type A personalities tend to have greater blood pressure reactions than type B personalities. This conclusion is based on a meta-analysis carried out by Scott Lyness on nearly 100 studies.[17] Interestingly, the data suggest that persons with Type A personalities seemed to react most when they were in competitive situations, or knew that their performances were being evaluated.

An Extension of Type A to Behavior Behind the Wheel

In describing the free-floating hostility component of Type A behavior, Friedman and Ulmer related an anecdote concerning one of their hostile Type A patients.[18] Driving in his car, the patient stopped for a red light. While waiting for the light to change he lit a cigarette. The light turned green. Before he had finished, a woman in the car behind him honked several times. Rather than drive on, the man got out of his car, smiled at her with a sneer, walked to the front of his car and opened the hood; he pretended that he was looking for a mechanical breakdown. Later he told a friend, "I think the bitch got the message."

There are empirical links between Type A behavior and aggressive driving behavior. James Elander and his colleagues have reviewed some of these data.[19] Questionnaire measures of Type A behavior have been statistically related to crash rates, self-reports of fast driving, more frequent braking, passing, horn use and driver impatience.

An association between measures of aggression and automobile crashes was reported in a study carried out by F.L. McGuire.[20] McGuire collected psychological data using tests and questionnaires from nearly 3,000 people applying for driving licenses. He followed the people for two years looking at their automobile accident records, finding that aggression and expression of hostile feelings was associated with crash involvement.

Looking at the issue of aggressive driving from a different perspective, researchers examined the driving records of a sample of incarcerated criminals. They found that the criminals were nearly six times as likely to have been involved in automobile accidents resulting in damage or injury than was the case for the general population. For accidents involving a fatality, the figure rose to almost 20 times as likely.[21]

Anger and Depression

Anger may be implicated in the development of psychological problems as well as physical ones. There is some evidence that anger may be involved in depression. The idea for this relation stems from Freud's essay, *Mourning and Melancholia*, in which Freud advanced the theory that anger generated by unrequited love may not be directed at the love object, but could be unconsciously turned inwardly against the self. Freud observed that such persons' statements were filled with self-reproach, self-accusations and feelings of worthlessness.[22]

While Freud postulated a relation between anger-turned-inward and depression in the context of romantic disappointment, the relation strikes me as more general than that. I would hypothesize that when a person becomes angry with himself or herself for whatever cause, there is an increased risk of the person feeling depressed.

A number of studies support this view. Several researchers have found correlations between reports of anger and depression. Roland Tanck and I found that on days when college students reported feeling angry, they were much more likely to also report feeling depressed than on days in which they did not feel angry. We also found that students who had directed anger against themselves had higher levels of depression than students who did not direct anger against themselves.[23]

Aggressiveness

Like anger, aggressiveness can have effects that are useful and adaptive, and like anger, it has a dark side that can be destructive. Novaco described aggression as "inevitably learned behavior because of its instrumental value."[24] The case for aggressiveness in the survival of the human species is straightforward and requires little imagination. During the ice ages, men hunted huge mammoths for food, not a task for the fainthearted. Even in today's civilized world aggressiveness is of value in the pursuit of success, wealth and a mate. A person who is overly passive may end up with none of the above.

In our view, self defense is a form of aggressive behavior. Whether it is a child protecting himself from a schoolyard bully or a C.E.O. fending off a hostile corporate takeover, self interest requires the ability to fight back. The survival of the Western democracies and their Russian allies in their life and death struggle with Nazi Germany in World War II depended on their ability to outproduce the Nazis with weapons of war and to defeat them on the battlefield. Perhaps the ultimate parable for the fate of the defenseless lies in H.G. Wells' novel *The Time Machine*, where in a hypothetical distant future, the human race has split into two groups, a placid, hapless people who were fed by another people who used them as we now use livestock—they fattened them and ate them.[25]

While aggression can be adaptive, it can have an enormous downside. The Second World War left some 50,000,000 casualties in its wake. In writing about aggression, Novaco noted, "It is always in need of regulation because of its capacity to erode the social fabric."[26] Even when aggression is regulated by law and custom and when times are peaceful, aggressive acts can still cause problems both for the perpetrator and the person who is the target.

Children who are disruptive in class and bully their classmates are often rejected by their peers and become unpopular and lonely. When adults exchange angry words, the incident often sours the relationship. A study by Roy Baumeister and his colleagues makes the point clearly.[27] Undergraduate students were asked to describe an incident in which someone provoked them, making them really angry. The students' descriptions of these incidents were then evaluated to see if the incident had any negative consequences. In 73 percent of the narratives, the incident resulted in negative consequences. Damage to the relationship was noted in more than half of the accounts, and more than one-third of the students were still angry about what happened when they related their stories.

Aggressive acts have consequences and repeated aggressive acts are likely to have a cumulative effect. Such acts may generate hostility, fear and avoidance in the targets. We see the destructive effects of frequent aggressive acts in both family life and intimate relation-ships. The Warner family is an example. Bill Warner is a very bright man in his mid–30s. If he has a problem in life, it is that he abhors confrontations with other people and will do almost anything to avoid them. In contrast, his wife Anne often explodes in angry out-bursts directed against her coworkers, their teenage daughter and most of all, against Bill. In his passivity, Bill had created a vacuum and his wife has rushed to fill it. She constantly berates him, point-ing out his faults. Sometimes, she screams at him. At times she has physically attacked him. The situation has gotten so bad that their daughter has threatened to run away. Bill now feels like he is in a box, not knowing what to do. He has thought of leaving Anne but is concerned about his daughter. He feels depressed, is smoking heav-ily, suffers from indigestion, and often feels weak, tired and dizzy.

Violence Between Intimates

In the Warner household, it was the wife who committed acts of violence. For minor acts of aggression (pushing and shoving), women are probably as likely to engage in such behavior as their male partners. When violence between men and women is more seri-ous, where there are bruises and fractures, it is the male who usu-ally is the perpetrator. In commenting on major acts of domestic violence, the Department of Justice reported that "On average each year, women experienced over 572,000 violent victimizations com-mitted by an intimate, compared to approximately 49,000 incidents committed against men."[28] This is a ratio of more than ten to one.

In a report on the incidence of domestic violence, the Depart-ment of Justice used the more inclusive term "violence between inti-mates."[29] The term not only deals with violence between spouses, it also covers violence perpetrated by ex-spouses and lovers or by cur-rent lovers, boyfriends or girlfriends. The problem of intimate vio-lence is documented with pages of illustrative incidents in an October 1992 report of the majority staff of the Senate Judiciary Committee, Violence Against Woman: A Week in the Life of America.[30] In some of these incidents, the violence of husbands against wives was severe. In a community in Texas a woman was threatened with a gun by her husband of 18 years. He slapped her around, threatened to kill her, then hit her with the butt of a gun, knocking her unconscious while she lay bleeding. In a city in Florida, a mother of two young children was cooking in the kitchen when her husband returned from work and attacked her. He put her head in the sink and began beating her in the face with his fists. He dragged her through the house by her hair while telling her he was smart enough not to leave any bruises. He bragged that he would hurt her without leaving evidence.

Ex-spouses and former lovers and boyfriends can be equally brutal. In Connecticut, a 29-year-old woman was assaulted with an axe by her former husband, who threatened to kill her and then raped her. In the same state, a 30-year-old woman was walking her two-year-old child home from school. Her ex-boyfriend, the child's father, followed her home, forcing his way into the house. He beat her, raped her, then burnt the child's nose hairs with a cigarette lighter. At the time of the incident, the woman had a protective order against him.

Current boyfriends contribute their share to the stories of battering. In a case in Colorado, a man assaulted his girlfriend in a fast food restaurant. He pulled her hair, throwing her to the ground. She escaped and called the police. In a more harrowing incident in Vermont, a woman was vacationing with her live-in boyfriend. They were in or near a boat—it's not clear from the report—but he grabbed her head and beat it repeatedly against the side of the boat. Then he threw her into the water and attempted to drown her, choking her and holding her head under the boat. When she was admitted to the hospital, she had head wounds, two black eyes, a swollen lip and bruises on her neck and arms, and her kneecap was fractured.

How widespread is violence between intimates? The National Crime Victimization Survey carried out from 1987 to 1991 reported an annual average of more than 600,000 incidents of intimate violence (assaults, rapes or robberies).[31] The lion's share (81 percent) of violent acts committed by spouses and ex-spouses were assaults. It is clear that assaults against intimates are occurring in very large numbers. Department of Justice statistics suggest that about 2,000 of these incidents are acts of ultimate violence—murder.

Younger women—in the age range of 20 to 34—experience higher rates of intimate violence than older women. Income and education also make a difference: women who are college graduates experience less intimate violence than women who are less educated.

Women near the bottom of the economic ladder (family incomes less than $9,999) were more than five times as likely to experience intimate violence than women with family incomes exceeding $30,000.[32]

For some women, being assaulted by their husbands or boyfriends becomes a pattern of abuse. The Justice Department noted that "about 1 in 5 females victimized by their spouse or ex-spouse reported to the NCVS [National Crime Victimization Survey] that they had been a victim of a series of 3 or more assaults in the last 6 months that were so similar that they could not distinguish one from another."[33]

The majority of the injuries women incur in these violent episodes are not severe or life-threatening. About 54 percent of the women received injuries characterized as "minor." Still, there are numerous instances in which the injury was serious enough to require hospitalization. In the NCVS survey, 15 percent of the women went to hospitals after the assault.

Assertiveness Training

Aggressiveness can have positive value for an individual living in a competitive society such as our own. Aggression also has a downside, that if not kept within acceptable limits it can have serious, sometimes dire consequences for the individual and those around him. An attempt to dull the sharp edges of aggressive behavior, to moderate it—to tame the tiger into a useful personal and social commodity—has led to an interest in a realm of behavior called "assertiveness" and to a cottage industry called assertiveness training.

Have you ever seen a state flag with a coiled serpent pictured on it along with the motto, "Don't tread on me"? The flag is a metaphor for much of what we think of as assertiveness. The assertive person is not going to be a patsy, someone who is pushed around. Assertive people will stand up for their rights. These are not academic considerations. Being pushed around may be something trivial but annoying, such as an incident that occurred in a bank line where a woman shoved herself in front of a friend of mine, or something chronically irritating such as the circumstances of a patient of mine whose roommate had no respect for her and constantly told her what to do.

The other major aspect of assertiveness has to do with not being shy about going after what one wants. The assertive person has overcome any reluctance to speak out in the classroom. The assertive male pursues that attractive woman he sees and is not hesitant about asking her out. The assertive person applies for the desirable job and looks confident in the interview. On the job, he pushes for a promotion. In the pursuit of goals—short term and long term—the assertive person does not hang back; he or she goes for them. The assertive credo holds that the admonition that it is unseemly to put oneself forward is a good motto—for someone else. If not overdone, and this is very easy to do, assertiveness is not a bad prescription for someone desirous of enjoying success in our competitive, market-driven society. Certainly, for those people who are shy and timid, being more assertive could make a difference in their lives.

Where there are niches to be filled, there are entrepreneurs. And so we had the development of assertiveness training. How does one do assertiveness training? One way is to use a variant of social skills training, a method developed by psychologists interested in behavioral modification. The method involves presentation of models of the behavior desired, coaching and role playing. The instructor might present a hypothetical situation to the client, ask how the client would respond in such a situation, offer a better alternative, try role-playing the situation, then critique the client's performance.

Here is a hypothetical situation that is similar to situations used by assertiveness training. You are at a very fancy restaurant with your date. You have been waiting a long time to be served. You notice that other couples that came into the restaurant after you have been waited on. You see that the waiter is about to pass by your table again. You speak to the waiter and say ... What?

If the client's statement is weak and ineffectual, the trainer offers something stronger as a model, perhaps something like, "We've been waiting a very long time to have our order taken. Other people have come into the restaurant after us and you've waited on them. Are you going to take our order now, or do you want me to speak to the manager?"

Sometimes people are not only unassertive but have an acute fear of being in a situation where they may have to take assertive action. As an example, consider dating behavior. Some men are terrified at the idea of asking a woman for a date. The discomfort level may be so high that simply teaching these men assertive social skills is not likely to work very well. An alternative is to try to reduce the patient's anxiety level first, and then try role playing exercises afterwards.

One procedure a therapist can try to use is called "systematic desensitization." The patient is first taught the skill of deep muscle relaxation. Then while the patient is relaxed, he is asked to visualize in his mind a series of scenes that gradually increase the threat level to the patient. When the patient is able to visualize the scenes without feeling anxious, he may be able to more easily enter into the role playing exercises.

Here is an example of dating-related scenes that I have used with shy male patients. The patients visualized these scenes while relaxed:

1. There is a dance being held tonight at the _____. You are thinking about possibly going. You decide to give it a try.

2. You are standing outside the door of the dance floor. You can hear a band playing songs you recognize.

3. You walk inside and pay the entrance fee. You look around and see a number of people dancing.

4. You see three or four women who are alone. You notice a woman about your age who is standing by herself. She looks like a pleasant person.

5. You walk over to her. You say, "Hi. My name is _____. Would you like to dance?"

6. She smiles and nods. You walk with her to the dance floor.

7. You are dancing with her. In awhile, you experience a pleasant sensation dancing with her.

8. You tell her you enjoyed dancing with her. You ask her whether she'd like to sit down and talk awhile.

9. You are seated together. You ask her about the kind of work she does and the kind of things she enjoys doing.

When a patient has been desensitized in the therapist's office and has practiced dating skills in role-playing, will he then use these skills in the real world, or will nothing really change? In the last analysis, the patient has to overcome that psychological barrier himself. Phobic reactions can be very powerful and not everyone will succeed.

So we have seen that extremes on either side of the scale measuring aggressiveness can have negative consequences. The big difference is that uncontrolled aggressiveness is likely to hurt other people, perhaps severely, while extreme passivity is most damaging to oneself.

CHAPTER 6

Violence and the Media

O n a late March day in 1998, the nation was shocked by a news
report from Jonesboro, Arkansas. Two boys, 13 and 11 years
old, had ambushed their classmates by setting off a fire alarm, then
gunned them down after they emerged from the school. The incident occurred in the wake of another school shooting in West Pad-
ucah, Kentucky, in which students in a prayer group were killed by
a fellow student, and was followed in May by an equally tragic
shooting incident in Springfield, Oregon. The spate of school shootings with multiple victims included communities in Tennessee, South
Carolina, Florida, Kansas, Missouri and Colorado.[1]

After the Arkansas, Oregon and Colorado shootings, journal-
ists, commentators and experts of various sorts were on the airways
trying to explain to a bewildered public how it was possible that such
young children could commit such a callous crime. High among the
list of suspects was the influence of the mass media, particularly
television and movies. The assertion that violence portrayed on television was partly to blame for these violent acts was seldom questioned. The media is presently held in low regard and almost
everyone has seen episodes of both factual and fictional violence on
television and in the movies. Surely, it was reasoned, repeated exposure to such graphic violence would have an impact on children.

The possible role of the media in promoting violence has been a matter of considerable public concern for several decades. Almost 15 years ago, Jonathan Freedman wrote a review of research on television and violence that began, "Whether viewing violence on television affects aggressive behavior is a widely discussed question. It appears in virtually every introductory textbook, every text in social psychology and developmental psychology, and in many articles and reports. Moreover, it has serious implications for social policy, as well as for child rearing and perhaps for criminology."[2] One of the references cited by Freedman, "TV Violence and Viewer Aggression: A Cumulation of Study Results 1956–1976," shows that this problem has a long history.[3]

The concerns of the public health community were formally expressed in 1972 in a report published by the Surgeon General's Scientific Advisory Committee on television and Social Behavior, titled *Television and Growing Up: The Impact of Televised Violence*. With some qualifications, the report concluded that the evidence supported a "preliminary and tentative indication of a causal relation between viewing violence on television and aggressive behavior."[4]

The argument that the mass media (principally television) promotes violence in everyday life is based on several assumptions: (1) television screens are replete with violent imagery; (2) children spend a large proportion of their time watching television; and (3) the impact of such viewing will influence the attitudes of children about the acceptability of violence and lower their thresholds for committing violent acts. When one investigates the validity of these assumptions, one finds considerable support for them. Projects have been undertaken at universities to monitor the incidence of violence in television programs. Students have been assigned the thankless job of watching television programs for hours on end and recording instances of violence. In a recent study (1998) about 2,000 people recorded instances of violence during 9,000 hours of television programming, monitoring 23 channels from early morning until 11:00 p.m.[5] It is clear from such studies that despite public outcries, there continues to be a substantial amount of violence portrayed on television. The violence begins with children's shows in the morning in which cartoon characters bludgeon one another, continues with the afternoon and evening news in which violent acts are often feature stories, and moves on to fictional shows about police and crime in which violence is a stock in trade.

Statistical data reporting on the frequency with which violent acts occur on television has been provided over many years by researchers led by George Gerbner.[6] Their analysis indicated that the level of violence in prime-time hours has run consistently at the rate of about five violent acts per hour. The rate of violence in children's Saturday morning shows was substantially higher, running around 20 to 25 violent acts per hour. A survey by the Center for Media and Public Affairs, considering all television programming including cable on a given day (April 7, 1994) in Washington, D.C., tallied 2,605 violent acts during that short time span.[7] The majority of the acts took place in the early morning when children were watching.

How much time do children spend watching television? Studies indicate that children begin watching television in infancy, and the amount of time spent watching television increases steadily through early and middle childhood, reaching a peak around 12 years of age. At about the age of 12, children tend to spend about four hours a day watching television.[8] This statement must be qualified in that during some of this time, the child may be only partially attentive to what is on the screen. He or she may be talking, eating or doing homework while the television set is on. Studies suggest that about 70 percent of the time the T.V. set is on, the 12-year-old child will watch it.

In commenting on these statistical data, Aletha Huston and her colleagues observed, "If we multiply these rates of televised violence by the amount of viewing of the average preschooler and school-aged child (two to four hours a day), we begin to understand the magnitude of the problem. By the time the average child graduates from elementary school, she or he will have witnessed at least 8,000 murders and more than 100,000 other assorted acts of violence. Depending on the amount of television viewed, our youngsters could see more than 200,000 violent acts before they hit the schools and streets of our nation as teenagers."[9]

Even if these estimates are exaggerated by a factor of two or five or even ten, it is clear that children are being exposed to huge amounts of violence on television. There is overwhelming evidence to support the first two assumptions, that there is a plethora of violence on the television screen and that children spend a large amount of time watching television. The crucial questions, then, become: Does watching television violence have an impact on children? Does watching television make them more tolerant of aggressive acts and more aggressive in their behavior?

In a number of early studies, researchers attempted to address the latter question with laboratory experiments. Children would be shown a film containing violent scenes. Afterwards, they would be given an opportunity to make an aggressive response such as shoving another child. The aggressive responses of these children were compared with those of control subjects who had watched a film that did not have violent scenes. In commenting on these studies, Freedman observed, "It seems clear that this work has demonstrated that viewing violent material on television or film in the laboratory can increase aggressive responses in the laboratory."[10]

The findings from such laboratory studies were provocative but they did not answer the question of how children respond to television violence in real life situations. To address this question, quasi-experimental studies were undertaken. Children (e.g., students in a residential school) were shown either aggressive or nonaggressive films. Then they were told to play with the other children. The children's play was observed unobtrusively by trained observers who noted evidence of aggressive activity. Wendy Wood and her colleagues evaluated the results of studies that employed such strategies, using the statistical technique of meta-analysis to provide an overall assessment of the results. Here is their conclusion. "Does exposure to media violence increase viewers' aggression? Our review of 28 experiments examining children's and adolescents' spontaneous aggression during unconstrained social interaction reveals that it does."[11] We should inject a cautionary note: the effect, while significant, was not particularly large and not all studies reported positive findings.

If, as this analysis indicates, viewing television violence promotes aggression, we might expect that people who watch a lot of television programming that included violence would be more aggressive than people who watch little such programming. Consider a representative study carried out by Leonard Eron and his colleagues.[12] They studied children in the third grade, looking at the relationship between the amount of television violence they viewed and how aggressive they were in the classroom. The researchers found a small positive relation between these measures for boys. When the researchers reassessed the children ten years later, they found that early exposure to television violence continued to have a statistical relation to aggression assessed in adolescence.

The findings from this study and similar studies buttress the findings from the experimental studies. Television violence is a factor in promoting aggressive behavior. The size of the effects found indicates that television viewing is probably not the primary reason for aggressive behavior. Still, it is part of the mix. One could imagine that for some, particularly susceptible children, television violence could have a powerful influence.

Watching violence on the television or movie screen not only has an influence on stimulating aggressive behavior, it may create a tolerance for aggressive behavior in others. After watching violence portrayed on the screen, children may be less likely to intervene to stop aggressive acts when they see them. Some experiments carried out by Ronald Drabman and Margaret Thomas in the mid–1970s were recently replicated by Fred Molitor and Kenneth Hirsch.[13] Fourth and fifth grade children saw either scenes from a film with violence (*The Karate Kid*) or nonviolent scenes from the Olympic Games. Then the children were shown by means of a video camera what appeared to be escalating attacks of a young boy and girl on each other in the adjoining room. The young children destroyed each other's play constructions—houses of building blocks, made verbal threats that they would strike each other and pushed and shoved each other. The children watching these aggressive acts on the video monitor had been previously instructed to watch the monitor, to keep an eye on the boy and girl, and if trouble developed to seek the researcher in the principal's office. The researcher actually stood in the hallway outside holding a stopwatch to note the amount of time it took for the children to leave the room and head for the principal's office. The children who watched *The Karate Kid* took longer to leave the room to notify the researcher of the altercation. While one must be cautious in interpreting these findings, it appears that exposure to violence can deaden its impact, a phenomenon that has been observed in inner city children living in violent environments.

The possible desensitizing effects of watching television violence was used as a defense (albeit unsuccessfully) in a murder trial held in Florida. A 15-year-old boy shot and killed his 82-year-old neighbor. In the trial, the boy's lawyer argued that his client should not be found guilty because he had become dangerously inured to violence from watching too much television: he was no longer able to tell right from wrong.[14]

Some children may not only become desensitized to watching violence, they may develop a preference for it. Mona El-Sheikh gave four- and five-year-old children a choice between watching two brief videotaped angry exchanges between adults. In one of the tapes, the people were described as "a little mad." In the other tape they were described as "very mad." About equal numbers of children asked to see the more intense and less intense adult arguments. In the actual experiment, all of the children watched the same videotapes. The researchers found that the children who said they wanted to see the more intense argument reported less distress from watching the tapes.[15] Interestingly, the preschool children who wanted to look at the tape showing more intense anger were more likely than the other children to have conduct problems.

That some children prefer to watch intense aggression rather than a more subdued version has its parallel with adults. Many adults will pay a premium fee to watch boxing matches in which a contestant may be knocked senseless. Many adults are avid fans of professional wrestling exhibitions in which the participants slam each other around in seemingly brutal combat. Perhaps the ultimate example of people seeking the opportunity to watch human beings bludgeon each other occurred in the Roman Colosseum. These bloody spectacles called "games" featured gladiatorial combat often to the point of death and people being torn apart by wild animals.

The games were not rare events. The Roman historian Tacitus noted that they had become one of the characteristic vices of the metropolis.[16] These spectacles could be exceptionally brutal. Contemporaneous accounts describe a man being disemboweled by a bear and 18 elephants being set upon a group of criminals.[17] One wonders whether the spectators of this slaughter yelled and cheered.

Who Reacts to Screen Violence by Becoming Aggressive?

It is obvious that not everyone who watches violence on the television and movie screens reacts by becoming aggressive. If this were the case, our society would be far more violent than it is. When we look for people who might have a tendency to react aggressively to televised violence, an obvious place to start is with people who are aggressive in everyday life. We know that aggressiveness is a characteristic of the individual that can be measured with psychological tests. We might expect that people who score high and low on these tests would differ in terms of their reactions to aggression portrayed on the screen. Research indicates that this is the case.

A recent set of experiments carried out by Brad Bushman at Iowa State University provides a good illustration of this tendency.[18] Bushman used a scale from Buss and Perry's Aggression Questionnaire as the measure of aggressiveness. In his first study, he gave the undergraduate students who served as subjects a series of written film synopses to examine. These descriptions were not synopses of actual films, but were contrived for the experiment. Some of the synopses described violent films, some nonviolent films. Here is an example of a synopsis for a violent film:

> Nicoline Chester isn't your average femme fatale. She's a hired killer who has a way with words. She even has the police fooled into believing her innocence. Lieutenant David Otello isn't convinced, though. He pursues her forcefully after she kills her uncle, only to learn that he's the next target. Their final confrontation leads them into the Dallas Museum of Natural History where a bloodbath ensues. Otello discovers that Nicoline won't let anyone get in the way of her work.[19]

Here is an example of a synopsis for a nonviolent film:

> Professor Bertilson and his 10-year-old son Bill depart from Boston on a voyage of exploration. They are sailing their schooner in uncharted waters when a typhoon strikes with sudden fury. The mountainous waves rip loose the topsail and fling their schooner into a line of breakers. The two manage to make it to shore, parched and groggy. Professor Bertilson and his only son are stranded on a lost island, where dinosaurs and people live together in peaceful interdependence. This film chronicles their exciting, and often spectacular, adventures.[20]

The students were told to read through the series of film synopses and pick one they wanted to watch. The students scoring higher on the Aggression Questionnaire were more likely to choose a violent film to watch than the students scoring lower on the questionnaire.

In a second experiment Bushman showed 15-minute sections of two actual films to college students, *Karate Kid III*, which contained violent scenes, and *Gorillas in the Mist*, which showed a scientist studying gorillas in their native habitat. This film did not contain scenes of overt violence. The students' reactions to viewing the films were assessed using an adjective check list. The students who scored higher on the Buss-Perry Aggression Questionnaire reacted to the violent film with more hostility on the adjective check list than the students with lower scores on the Aggression Questionnaire.

In a third study, Bushman again showed the films *Karate Kid III* and *Gorillas in the Mist* to groups of students. After the films the students were asked to take part in two-person reaction-time contests. The student who had the slower reaction time in each trial of the contest was to receive a blast of noise in his or her ear that sounds like radio static. The two contestants were asked to set the level of noise that their opponent would receive. In actuality, the researcher delivered noise to each of the opponents on 50 percent of the trials. The results showed that the students who had watched *Karate Kid III* set the noise levels higher than students who had watched *Gorillas in the Mist*. The students with higher scores on the Buss-Perry Aggression Questionnaire set the noise levels higher than students with lower scores on the questionnaire. Finally, students who reported that they spend considerable time watching violent television shows set higher levels of noise for their opponents than the students who watched violence on television less frequently.

Television and the Other Mass Media

Violence portrayed in the media did not begin with television. Shakespeare's 16th century plays *Hamlet* and *Macbeth* had large body counts among the principal characters. Naming the featured players who survived (there weren't many) would be a good trivia question for the literary buff. Violent stories on the printed page have a venerable history. I wonder what newspaper it was in colonial times that had the distinction of first reporting an act of murder or mayhem. For many years, magazines and books have printed stories that included violence. Recall stories about the Old West or detective thrillers from such authors as Raymond Chandler, Dashiell Hammett and Mickey Spillane. Motion pictures dating back to the westerns of the silent films have featured fist fights and fatal exchanges of gunfire. In the 1930s motion pictures portraying wanton killings were a Hollywood staple, with films like *The Roaring Twenties, Public Enemy,* and *Little Caesar* drawing crowds into the movie theaters. Many films of recent years have included violent scenes with the addition of color and special effects to make the imagery more compelling. A whole genre of movies, "martial art" films, have no other obvious *raison d'être* than to portray violence.

Radio, which was the prime center of home entertainment before the advent of television, had its share of mystery, detective and horror programs that usually included one or more murders in their 30 minutes (minus commercials) of air time. Radio had its Sam Spade, Richard Diamond and Ellery Queen tracking down murderers and Matt Dillon shooting down "the killers and the spoilers" around Dodge City. For an element of horror there were shows such as *The Shadow* and *Inner Sanctum*. Only the *Lone Ranger* had an unblemished record (as far as I know) of not killing anyone, having the unerring accuracy to shoot the guns out of the hands of the outlaws he faced.

Someone once said, "One picture is worth a thousand words." Even as a rough equation, this would help explain the preeminence of television among the media in its impact. To begin with, how many young people read a thousand words in a day? And how many television pictures do they see? For the typical youngster, it is clearly no contest.

Compare the clarity and vividness of the television picture with the words on the printed page. Once more there is no contest. The television picture is immediate, clear and direct, requiring little effort to comprehend its meaning. To decipher the printed word requires an active effort and more use of the imagination. While the growth of the Internet may change the picture, young people today spend many hours absorbing the vivid images of television and comparatively little time reading books and articles.

As is the case for reading books, radio dramatizations required the active involvement of the imagination. If radio portrayed a fist fight or an exchange of gunfire, the listener had to imagine the scene in his or her own mind. All the listener was likely to hear were a few sound effects, a line or two of speech and perhaps some grunts. From this limited array of cues, the listener had to project from his previous experience what might be happening. The listener could construct a scene that was rich in details or one that was nonspecific and bland. The option of minimizing the violent nature of the scene is less available to the television or movie viewer, as one sees the event in as much detail as the film director wishes to present. The singular impact of television among the mass media arises from the combination of thousands of hours of viewer exposure and the medium's direct portrayal of events.

The Context of Media Violence

Violence portrayed in the media, whether in television, movies or print, usually occurs in a context. The context may be minimal or it may be well laid out as in the intricate plot of a mystery novel. The context in which violence occurs can affect the way the act is interpreted and the impetus it can have toward stimulating aggression in the viewer.

In her book *Viewing Violence*, Madeline Levine discusses several contextual factors that could influence the reaction of viewers to the portrayal of violence on the screen.[21] One of these factors is realism. Levine posits that if the violent act is a real event (e.g., a bombing at a clinic, a shooting at a school) or appears real, it is likely to have more effect on stimulating aggression in the viewer than if the violent act is obviously faked or contrived. A film with huge body counts (e.g., *Robocop*) may be seen as overblown and unreal by the viewer and be less likely to elicit violence than more realistic films such as *Colors*. Evidence supporting this hypothesis comes in a study carried out by Seymour Feshbach in which children were shown a film of a riot. Some of the children were told that they were viewing a newsreel of a real event while the other children were told that they were watching a Hollywood movie. When the film was over, the children were given a chance to be aggressive (pushing a peer). The children who thought that they had watched a real event were more aggressive than the children who thought that they had watched a movie.[22]

A second factor that might influence children's reactions to violent films is whether the violent acts appear to be justified. Levine posits that if the violent act on the screen seems justified to the viewer, it is more likely to have the effect of fostering aggression in the viewer. There are historical parallels for this idea. During the Reign of Terror in the French Revolution, crowds were said to have jeered and cheered while members of the nobility who were perceived as longtime oppressors were guillotined. In Rwanda, the execution by firing squad of people convicted of participating in the genocide in that country was accompanied by the cheers of a large crowd. When a violent act is one of retribution, the act seems more acceptable, and may be more likely to promote aggression.

A film critic could easily draw up a list of movies in which violence is perpetuated as retribution. Clint Eastwood, Charles Bronson and Sylvester Stallone are among the well-known actors who have made films playing vigilantes executing their own form of violent, rough justice. Interestingly, in one of the classic novels of retribution, Alexandre Dumas' *The Count of Monte Cristo*, a full measure of retribution was exacted by the protagonist with minimum violence. While the level of violence in retribution films may seem excessive, it is apparently good box office.

The 1998 study monitoring television programming found that 40 percent of the violence on television was committed by good characters—heroes rather than villains. In about one-third of the shows, even the bad characters escape punishment. More than 70 percent of the aggressors—good, bad and ugly—show no remorse and experience no criticism or penalty.[23]

Drawing on a study carried out by M.A. Rosekrans, Levine noted that similarities between the portrayed aggressor and the viewer might increase the likelihood of an aggressive response by the viewer.[24] The idea is that it may be easier to identify with and model someone that is like you than someone who is clearly different.

Finally, Levine observed that the consequences (or lack of consequences) of the aggressive act can be important. If the child sees an aggressive act on television that causes pain, sorrow and suffering, he or she may empathize with the victim and feel less disposed to act aggressively than if the act had no consequences. If this analysis is correct, current television programming is not particularly helpful. In the 1998 study monitoring television programming, it was reported that in about half of the television episodes of violence recorded, there was no indication that anyone was hurt; there was no pain, suffering or physical injury.[25] Shows depicting long-term effects of violence on the victim, the family or the community were rare.

Have you ever seen one of those video games in which the participants engage in deadly combat? One of the criticisms of these games is that the participants can engage in destructive acts against each other and when the game is over, there are no observable consequences. Simply push a button and everything is back to normal. It is not inconceivable that very young children who come into possession of a firearm might not fully appreciate the difference between real life and the video game. They may think that everything can be just the way it was after they fire the gun.

The Controversy Over Song Lyrics

The popular music of the 1930s and 1940s had lyrics that were almost always about romantic love. The only songs from that era that attempted to stir up aggressive feelings were patriotic Second World War songs such as *Praise the Lord and Pass the Ammunition*. Following the advent of rock-and-roll in the 1950s, popular music has traveled in divergent pathways and some of the musical forms that emerged—heavy metal, rock videos and rap—have at times included lyrics that seem to extol violence.

An example of a rock video with violent imagery is *We're Not Gonna Take It* by Twisted Sister in which a boy hurls his father through a plate glass window.[26] Gangsta rap has included the much-criticized violent lyrics of *Cop Killer*. The defenders of rap argue that such violent messages are more reflections of life than the cause of violence in these communities. They argue that rap is a legitimate form of artistic expression. Granting that position, it is certainly possible for a legitimate form of expression to promote violence. A classic example is the novel *Uncle Tom's Cabin*, which had much to do with stirring up the passions that culminated in the American Civil War.

Controlling Television Violence

Self-restraint by the movie and television industries, placing limits on the amount of violence shown on the screen, is always a possibility. The industries could adopt codes that draw lines beyond which they will not traverse. There is a precedent for self-policing in the movie industry that once went to the extreme length of establishing a censorship office (the Hays Office) that kept any sexual activity beyond kissing off the screen. The reinstitution of such an office for self-censorship is unlikely and would be an anathema to people who value freedom of artistic expression.

Public boycotts of corporations that sponsor or produce violent television might have some effect. Corporations are protective of their public images. In the last analysis, however, it is the viewing audience that drives the content of movies and television programs. If box office receipts for a violent film are high, you are likely to see more of the same. Similarly, if audience ratings for a shoot-'em-up television series are high, expect to see copycat shows in the following season, if not sooner. Ultimately, what sells dominates the screen.

In an age of market-driven economies, self-restraint by the industries and public outcries may only have limited effects on curbing violence on the screen. For the foreseeable future, the major effort to limit children's exposure to screen violence is likely to come within the home.

Enter the V-chip

The hoped-for white knight to slay the dragon of television violence has the futuristic name of the "V-chip." The chip, invented by a Vancouver engineer, has the capability of blocking out television shows that have been coded as violent or being sexually explicit. Parents are expected to program the V-chip to perform this function.

Canada passed a law requiring that all television sets sold in that nation contain the V-chip. America followed Canada's lead. The 1996 Telecommunications Act included a provision that as of a set date, all new television sets must contain the V-chip. The task of implementing the legislation fell to the Federal Communications Commission (FCC). On March 12, 1998, the FCC announced in a press release the adoption of a voluntary rating system for television programming and the requirement that television sets must have the V-chip[27]:

> The Commission today adopted an order finding acceptable the video programming rating system currently in voluntary use and established technical requirements for consumer electronic equipment to enable blocking of video programming. These two actions will help provide parents with the information and ability to make informed viewing decisions for their families....
>
> The Commission finds that the Industry's *TV Parental Guidelines* establish acceptable voluntary rating rules.... In a companion item the Commission adopted technical rules that require television receivers with picture screens 33 centimeters (13 inches) or greater to be equipped with features to block the display of television programming with a common rating, commonly referred to as "v-chip" technology. The v-chip will be phased in with half of television receiver models with picture screens 33 cm or greater required to have the v-chip by July 1, 1999, and all such models required to have the v-chip by January 1, 2000.

A statement by the FCC Commissioner Gloria Tristani makes the case for these rules[28]:

> As I travel around the country, I hear again and again from parents who are concerned about what their children are being exposed to on TV. The facts support their concern. Children spend about 25 hours a week watching TV, more time each year than they spend in the classroom. And much of what they are watching is violent. By the time they complete elementary school, children have witnessed about 8,000 murders and 100,000 acts of violence.
>
> Parents want to protect their children from violent and other kinds of programming that they consider harmful. But the task is daunting. Nowadays there aren't just three channels to monitor, there are dozens. No parent can possibly know what's on all of them all of the time. And in this age of single parent families and families in which both parents must work to make ends meet, it simply isn't possible for parents to always be at home to monitor what their children are watching. These parents want and deserve the ability to protect their children as much as parents who are able to closely monitor their children's viewing habits.
>
> Today's actions will give parents a modern tool to help raise their children in the modern world. Under the voluntary Industry rating

system we have found acceptable, parents should be able to receive the information they need in order to determine whether an upcoming program contains sex, violence, offensive language or suggestive dialogue. When used in conjunction with the V-chip, parents will be able to prevent their children from viewing programming that they consider harmful, even when they cannot be home.

The V-chip will not relieve parents of the responsibility of determining what their children watch on TV. It will help them fulfill that responsibility. Those who urge parents to simply turn off the shows they do not want their children to see should welcome the V-chip. The V-chip is essentially a remote control device with a longer range. It allows parents to "turn off" programs that they believe are harmful to their children while they are at work, at a PTA meeting, or at a Saturday night movie. It will not be a substitute for parents; it will help parents do their jobs.

In the near future, parents buying television sets should be able to exercise more control over the level of violence their children will be exposed to on television. It will be interesting to see how parents use this new tool in practice and whether the introduction of this device will be eventually followed by measurable decreases in community violence. Comparisons of homes where the V-chip is fully utilized with those in which it is ignored (like unused seat belts) would be instructive. The possibilities for research are intriguing.

CHAPTER 7

Alcohol and Aggression

O God, that men should put an enemy in their mouths to
steal away their brains! That we should, with joy, pleasure,
revel and applause transform ourselves into beasts!
Othello, Act 2, Scene 3[1]

Shakespeare's 16th century commentary on drinking is as applicable today as when he wrote it. Still, the belief that alcohol can unleash antisocial and aggressive behaviors was not always widely held. In America, popular views about the effects of alcohol on behavior have undergone major shifts over the centuries. Historians tell us that in colonial days, alcohol was generally thought of as a helpful rather than harmful substance. The Puritan preacher Cotton Mather called liquor "the good creature of God."[2] It is said that during this era, Americans drank prodigiously, "from the crack of dawn to the crack of dawn."[3] They drank while they ate, worked, traveled and often between times. The major negative effect of alcohol was more likely to be seen as idleness than aggression. Acts of aggression were blamed more on the corrupting atmosphere of the local taverns where liquor was served than on the effects of the drink itself.

How different was the view of alcohol expressed in the 19th century. Barbara Critchlow describes the change in attitude succinctly. "Where colonial Americans believed that alcohol led to pleasant effects—relaxation, stimulation, pleasure—19th century Americans came to see these effects as tantamount to depravity."[4]

The 19th century temperance movement with all of its zeal and excesses correctly pointed out a link between alcohol and crime. Temperance advocate Samuel Chipman wrote in 1845: "The great mass of crime is justly attributable to this prolific parent of corruption ... the recklessness, the profligacy, and crime which people our jails, were the legitimate offspring of ardent spirits."[5] What colorful rhetoric! How drab our modern peer-reviewed journal articles would seem to Mr. Chipman. While Chipman's assessment of the association between alcohol and crime is overstated, one can see how far the pendulum had swung.

The current popular view of alcohol is that drinking may have a variety of effects on people. Among the characteristic reactions children (seventh graders) expect from intoxicated adults are meanness, loudness and aggressiveness.[6] College students expect social drinkers to become more relaxed, kinder, sloppier, louder and more aggressive.[7] So from an early age, people see aggressiveness as one of the possible outcomes from drinking. In many cases, this perception is based on bitter personal experience.

Some Clinical Vignettes

In my therapy practice it was not unusual to hear patients relate stories of how their parents, spouses and boyfriends had drunk too much, then became hostile, sometimes violent. A man in his 40s told me about his childhood—how his father used to work in the coal mines of West Virginia, get drunk on weekends, then come home in a rage. As a child, my patient was fearful and hid from his father. His story brings to mind D.H. Lawrence's portrait of the coal-mining father in *Sons and Lovers*.

A woman barely out of her teens talked about her father, a lawyer who had a long history of alcoholism. When he was drunk, he became verbally abusive to his wife, demeaning and disparaging her. Sometimes he would shove her around. When he was sober, he could be nice to his wife and his children, but when he was drunk, he was a horror. Finally, his wife couldn't stand it anymore, took the children and left.

A woman in her early 20s was married to a man who was quiet and passive. In contrast, she was quick tempered; she vented her angry feelings readily at him. After one of these exchanges, her husband would go to a bar. When he returned half-drunk, he called her a "whore," a "bitch" and a few other choice names. She knew that her own explosiveness was bringing most of this on, but she couldn't stop herself.

A divorced woman in her late 20s met a very good-looking man at a party, the kind of man she always wanted. After a few dates, she moved into his apartment. She soon found that he was a heavy drinker. Sometimes while drinking he would become withdrawn. At other times, he would become violent. Once he smashed down the door, threw her onto the floor and kicked her.

Drinking, Conflict and Violence

In writing about the effects of alcohol, researcher Claude Steele related an anecdote about a man he called Ted.[8] During a business trip, he had met Ted in a bar. Ted had been drinking heavily. A man came into the bar and made some remarks Ted found irritating. But in spite of the fact that Ted was well under the influence, he kept his cool and there was no sign of trouble. Two days later, there was a reprise of the scene. Steele met Ted at the bar; Ted had been drinking heavily. Once again the man who had made the irritating remarks approached them. He began to reiterate the things he said the previous night. This time, Ted reacted with rage. He shoved the man to the floor and stomped out of the bar.

Steele related this story to illustrate a point. The effects of alcohol on social behavior are unpredictable. Sometimes drinking leads to an excessive reaction, sometimes not.

Steele advanced the hypothesis that excessive social reactions that follow drinking are more likely to occur when the individual has a psychological conflict between carrying out some act (e.g., aggressive behavior, sexual behavior, risk taking) and inhibitions prohibiting such behavior. Steele proposed that when this psychological struggle was intense, the response to drinking would more likely be excessive. When Steele examined research data published by previous investigators, he found that much of the data seemed consistent with this formulation.

Steele's ideas bring to mind a spring that's wound too tight and when released does so with great force. Does the model apply to all episodes of alcoholic release? Probably not. There are people who drink with little inhibition and are aggressive much of the time. Nonetheless, it is an interesting formulation trying to understand people whose reactions go far beyond acceptable limits.

The Varied Effects of Drinking

It is important to put the effects of drinking on aggression into context. As Steele pointed out and popular thinking suggests, drinking is not followed by a single type of predictable behavior. Rather, drinking may be followed by a range of behaviors of which aggressive acts are but one kind. A study carried out by Kai Pernanen in taverns in a Canadian community illustrates this point well.[9] Pairs of trained observers recorded the actions of customers in 28 local taverns for about 600 hours. The observers recorded running accounts of behavior at randomly selected tables where two or more people were seated and drinking. By far the most frequently observed behavior was laughing. This was observed by one or more persons in 78 percent of the groups.

Next in order of frequencies were shaking hands (22 percent), backslapping (16 percent), playful aggressive behavior (16 percent), bragging, showing off (13 percent), and quarreling and arguing (10 percent). Pushing, shoving and physically aggressive behavior occurred in the three to four percent range. At times acts of verbal and physical aggression following drinking coexisted with gestures of friendly and affectionate behavior. The effects of drinking are complex and not all that predictable.

Alcohol and Spouse Battering

Some of the stories I related about drinking and violence had to do with wife-battering. Drinking and wife-battering is an all-too-common occurrence, but it would be a mistake to assume that all wife-batterers are heavy drinkers. Far from it. The reasons for battering are varied, including physical causes (e.g., some of these men may have sustained head injuries), as well as a range of psychological difficulties. Still, for many batterers, excessive drinking is part of the picture. Most studies carried out on this problem have found that men who abused their wives were more likely than nonviolent men to abuse alcohol.

L. Kevin Hamberger and James Hastings gave standardized tests to male spouse abusers, looking for signs of psychopathology.[10] They compared spouse abusers who abused alcohol with spouse abusers who did not. The test results suggested that the alcohol abusers had more severe psychopathology; they were more anxious and depressed and were more likely to distort and personalize perceptions of environmental events.

Based on their findings, Hamberger and Hastings drew a portrait of the violent wife abuser whose explosive reactions are potentiated by alcohol. He is a withdrawn, not very social person. He is inclined to be moody, hypersensitive to slights, and tends to overreact to personal stresses. His wife may describe him as volatile. When he perceives a real or imaginary slight, he may react violently—his reaction heightened by heavy drinking.

Using different psychological tests supplemented by interviews, David Saunders studied 165 wife batterers.[11] Analysis led him to draw a different portrait of the wife-battering, alcoholic abuser. Saunders' wife-batterer was more likely than not to have been severely abused as a child. Unlike Hamberger and Hastings' portrait, Saunders' wife-battering alcohol abusers were not likely to be very depressed. What distinguished Saunders' men is that they were generally violent—they not only battered their wives, they become involved in altercations elsewhere. They had a high arrest rate for drunken driving and violence.

Both of these profiles are of men who drink heavily and batter their wives. But the men showed different patterns of behavior and seemed like different types of people. As researchers have suggested, there is probably no single type of personality profile that can be used to describe all wife batterers. Alcohol does not enter the equation of wife-battering in an invariant way. A man might sit at home drinking, building up a case against his wife or he could come home drunk, already having had his share of fights. In either case, he can put his wife in the hospital.

Even when there is no physical aggression in a drunken episode between spouses—only hurtful and hostile words spoken—the damage to the relationship can be considerable. The excuse sometimes offered by the offending party may be, "I didn't really mean it—it was the alcohol." If there was a perceived transgression, it wasn't the person's fault. Drinking not only promotes aggression, but serves as an excuse for it.

Alcohol and Violent Crime

Alcohol consumption has been linked to the commission of a variety of violent crimes. A significant percentage of people who have committed murder, assault and rape were drinking before the violence ensued. A 1961 review by J.M. MacDonald of studies of murders indicated that about half of the people who had committed a homicide had been drinking before the killing.[12] More recent estimates continue to report high rates of alcohol involvement in murder and other violent crimes. "Making the Link," a fact sheet published by the Public Health Services Office of Substance Abuse Prevention, presented some damning statistics. Here are some examples. "Alcohol is a key factor in up to 68 percent of manslaughters, 62 percent of assaults, 54 percent of murders/attempted murders, 48 percent of robberies, and 44 percent of burglaries."[13] "Among jail inmates, 42.2 percent of those convicted of rape reported being under the influence of alcohol or alcohol and other drugs at the time of the offense."[14] A 1995 review of research linking alcohol and sexual aggression carried out by Michael Seto and Howard Barbaree suggests the figure may be even higher—in the 50 to 60 percent range.[15] In regard to domestic violence, a study that included more than 2,000 American couples reported that rates of domestic violence were nearly 15 times higher in households where husbands were often drunk as opposed to never drunk.[16]

The link between alcohol consumption and violent crime is not confined to the United States; it is international. Studies have confirmed this association in Finland, Kenya and Sweden. In Sweden, alcohol involvement in homicide may run as high as 80 percent of the cases.[17]

Studying the Effects of Alcohol on Aggressive Behavior

Such statistics provide overwhelming evidence of a relationship between alcohol consumption and aggressive behavior. To more closely study the effects of alcohol on behavior, researchers have used the experimental method, carrying out studies both in naturalistic settings and controlled laboratory settings. Here is an example of a study conducted in a naturalistic setting.

The men who participated in the study were assigned to one of three groups. Those who would drink: (1) hard liquor; (2) beer; or (3) non-alcoholic beverages. The men met in a comfortable room of a modern office building. They were free to order drinks from a bar throughout the evening although they were restricted to the assigned types of beverages. The participants spent their time playing darts, cards or shooting dice. At different points during the evening, the behavior of the men was videotaped. Aggressive-behavior scores were later calculated for each participant by analysts reviewing the tapes. The men who drank alcohol were evaluated as more aggressive than the men who consumed non-alcoholic beverages. The men who drank hard liquor were evaluated as more aggressive then the men who drank beer—and this aggressiveness seemed to increase as the evening wore on.[18]

In laboratory studies researchers have studied the effects of alcohol on aggression in controlled environments where both the intake of alcohol and the level of aggressiveness can be more precisely measured. In some of these experiments, participants were led to believe that they were in competition with an opponent in a reaction-time task. Moreover, during the experiment, the research subjects were instructed to use a device that would inflict discomfort (e.g., loud noise, electric shock) onto the other person, if the other person was slower. The subject was told before each trial that he will set the level of pain he will inflict. At the end of each trial, the subject was informed of the level of pain (e.g., shock) that his opponent had ostensibly set for him to receive. In reality, the experimenter determined who won and lost and the level of shock that was actually administered. The critical measure of aggression is the intensity of shock the subject sets for his opponent. And the critical finding for the experiment is whether alcohol affects this decision.

In examining the results of 30 studies using this or similar procedures, Brad Bushman and Harris Cooper concluded that "The evidence ... indicates that alcohol does indeed cause aggressive behavior."[19] They further stated, "Alcohol also appears to influence aggressive behavior as much or more than it influences other social and nonsocial behaviors.... Thus alcohol and aggression effects are by no means trivial.[20]

Why does the consumption of alcohol increase the likelihood of aggressive acts? No one is precisely sure at this time but several explanations have been offered. One widely held view is that alcohol acts to decrease inhibitions. Most of us have heard about instances of this, not only for aggressive behavior but for sexual behavior as well. It has been suggested that this disinhibition occurs by "anesthetizing the center of the brain" that normally inhibits aggressive behavior.[21] Another view is that drinking diminishes intellectual functioning, the ability to reason and pay attention. The person operates at an impaired level with reduced awareness, forethought and judgment. Claude Steele and Robert Josephs have labeled the effects of alcohol on thought and perception "alcohol myopia."[22] Under the influence, a person is less likely to pay attention to important environmental cues (the words, actions and expressions of others) that would normally give him or her pause to consider and desist.

Some theorists have noted that drinking often occurs in crowded, noisy, smoke-filled surroundings—aversive environments that could elicit aggression without alcohol use. They would argue that these circumstances elicit aggressive acts as much as the drinking. However, one can point out that there is no shortage of solitary, mean drinkers who become verbally and physically aggressive.

There is also the possibility of an expectation effect. The relationship between alcohol and aggressive behavior is widely recognized. People (including drinkers) have expectations that heavy drinking may lead to certain types of behavior such as increased sociability, sexual arousal and aggressive acts, and that these expectations may be self-fulfilling. Research using real and mock alcoholic beverages has found that people who think they are consuming an alcoholic drink (when they are not) do report more sexual arousal, but there is little evidence that they act more aggressively.[23]

The Other Side of the Coin

While alcohol abuse can lead to assaultive behavior, for women, being assaulted can lead to alcohol abuse. When a woman is beaten up or raped, she may react to this trauma by increased use of alcohol or drugs as a way of coping with the psychological pain induced by the assault. A team of researchers led by Dean Kilpatrick followed several thousand women over a period of two years, finding that women who had been physically or sexually assaulted during the study period had an increased risk of becoming alcohol abusers.[24] Moreover, other studies indicate that a history of being sexually abused increases the risk of developing an alcohol dependency problem.[25]

Alcohol and illicit drugs may become part of a relationship culture in which a man and woman abuse each other and also abuse substances, both as an instigator to aggressive behavior and as a way of coping with abuse. In a large study of young adults carried out in New Zealand, both perpetrators and victims of severe partner violence reported more symptoms of alcohol dependence and used more types of illegal drugs than people who were not involved in such violence.[26]

CHAPTER 8

When Communities Run Amok

S ometimes individuals become violent. Sometimes groups of peo- ple become violent. In a relatively tepid form, one sometimes sees this in an otherwise peaceful baseball game, when suddenly many players who have been sitting on the bench dash out on the field and start pushing and shoving members of the opposing team, even engaging in fist fights. These bench-clearing melees are infrequent events. They typically happen as the result of a clear-cut transgres- sion such as a pitcher throwing at the batter's head instead of over the plate. When the melee is over and the pitcher is warned by the umpire—or perhaps ejected from the game—the game continues. If there are more such incidents over time, "bad blood" may develop between the teams, lowering the threshold for future bench-clearing brawls.

Bloody riots that wreak havoc in communities share some ele- ments in common with baseball's bench-clearing melees. Both are initiated by a precipitating (triggering) event. In some cases this pre- cipitating event may be viewed as one that has gone beyond the limit, as constituting an intolerable act. It is not just a routine perceived misdeed; it is perceived as a flagrant act, even an outrage. In other cases, the precipitating event may not have been perceived as all that unusual; it was simply the latest in a chain of similar events—the straw that finally broke the camel's back.

In some riots, the precipitating event never actually occurred. People reacted to an unsubstantiated allegation or a rumor that greatly distorted the actual event. For example, in the early years of the republic (1819) in Philadelphia, thousands of people gathered to watch a balloon ascension. To get a close look, a person had to pay a dollar admission. Large numbers of people could not afford this and had to watch behind a fence. A false rumor circulated that a boy had been injured by a watchman who discovered the child climbing the fence. The story generated anger in the crowd, which surged forward, broke down the fence, tore the balloon to pieces and burned the pavilion.[1]

Whether people witness an actual event or simply believe that the event occurred, the situation gives rise to intense anger. Anger is followed by violent acts and then, importantly, social contagion. Other people begin to emulate the behavior of the initial participants, doing much the same thing. Indeed, some rioters may egg on others; the violence spreads and escalates in intensity. When large numbers of people break the rules there arises a sense among the participants that the rules no longer apply. Laws seem suspended. The actions of the growing mob become, at least temporarily, the prevailing social standard. People who never stole in their lives may begin to loot stores with a sense of impunity and little guilt. If everybody is doing it, why not? It must be okay! The ugliness of a riot may at times be tempered with a carnival-like atmosphere.

The analogy between baseball's bench-clearing melees and riots in a community holds only briefly. The loss of control evident on the baseball diamond quickly subsides; the disputants are separated by the umpires and players who have remained calm. In contrast, riots in the community may last several days with grievous downsides including deaths, injuries and destruction of property.

While the outbreak of tempers on the athletic field may have no obvious antecedents before the immediate triggering event, riots seldom erupt in a vacuum. Rather, there is a history of stored perceptions and beliefs that provide fuel when the spark is lit. In the memories of the participants, there is a black box of rage-reaction potential, much like the mental file cabinet of grievances unhappy partners in a marriage store up against one another that ultimately generates explosions.

Two types of belief systems underpin many riots. The first is the mind set that "I and people like me have been oppressed, that we have been treated unfairly." The mind set may include a litany of perceived misdeeds, transgressions and unfair acts and practices, punctuated by a sense of relative deprivation. The belief system typically expands to hold that others (defined by social class, ethnicity, gender, race, etc.) have it better than we do—and that they have taken actions to keep us deprived. If pushed to the extreme, the belief system borders on a conspiracy theory. When activated by a triggering event, the belief system may generate intense anger.

The second variant of the belief system that has engendered riots is one held by people who perceive themselves to be in the privileged rather than subordinate social position. The belief system is a complex of attitudes that includes disdain for those who are less privileged, often accompanied by fear of the very same people. The disdain is often based on negative attitudes communicated by one's parents during childhood that have been reinforced by one's peers and widely held social stereotypes. The fears that can be deep-seated include the possibility of economic competition and loss, possible retaliation from those who have been disadvantaged, and in the case of race riots, fears and loathing relating to inter-group sexual contacts.

Examples of Riots

Case I: The Belief System Is One of Being in an Oppressed Group

The United States has been a land of opportunity for millions of people who felt socially, religiously and economically disadvantaged in their homelands. Emigration to the United States has been the wellspring of countless success stories with great benefits for the individuals involved and the nation as a whole. In this context, however, one can point out groups of Americans who can make a good case that their forebears experienced social and economic discrimination. A few of the more obvious examples are Native Americans, African Americans and Chinese Americans for whom discriminatory practices went beyond exclusions imposed by customs and mores and were codified into law. Irish immigrants were greeted with signs stating "No Irish Need Apply" and Jewish Americans were prevented by restrictive covenants from moving into certain neighborhoods. Many immigrant groups who arrived at our shores with strange-sounding names, darker skin colors and foreign languages went through experiences that were a far cry from what was promised in Emma Lazarus' famous verse:

> Give me your tired, your poor,
> Your huddled masses yearning to breathe free,
> The wretched refuse of your teeming shore.[2]

Inspired by the American dream, the great majority of people who had experienced hostility, deprivation and discrimination continued to work within the system—getting an education and working hard to achieve prosperity. At times, however, the belief of being treated unfairly provided the impetus for violence.

CHICAGO, MAY 1886

The city of Chicago had been the site of large meetings protesting the status of workers in the rapidly industrializing American economy. The meetings were held against the backdrop of labor unrest in various parts of the country, including some incidents of violence. In late April, the Central Labor Union in Chicago held an eight-hour demonstration attended by some 25,000 people. On May 1, workers of all kinds—metal workers, brewers, tailors, carpenters and clerks—left their jobs. They held meetings and listened to speeches. Eighty thousand people marched arm-in-arm along Michigan Avenue.[3]

Some of the rhetoric these workers heard on May Day was very likely inflammatory. Included among the labor leaders were anarchists who advocated the destruction of capitalism and believed that bombs and bullets were the way to do it. Trouble was expected. Perched on rooftops along the parade route were policemen, Pinkerton operatives and deputized civilians armed with Winchester rifles. In armories the militia waited armed with Gatling guns. While there was nervous anticipation, the day turned out to be a peaceful exercise of First Amendment rights. It looked as if the city had escaped serious trouble.

On Chicago's Blue-Island Avenue stood the McCormick Reaper Works, which was turning out the machines revolutionizing American farming. Cyrus McCormick, Jr. had been engaged in a prolonged dispute with his workers. A recent strike had forced him to restore a 15 percent wage cut and McCormick was determined to break the union. He purchased machinery that eliminated the jobs of the skilled iron molders, who had led the strike. Then, he locked out the rest of his workers, replacing them with non-union labor. McCormick hired 300 armed Pinkerton men to protect these replacement workers.

During the spring the fired employees picketed the McCormick plant. The Pinkerton men and mounted police often clashed with the Pickets. Mounted police were said to have used billy clubs to disperse gatherings of Pickets. It was two days after the peaceful May Day March that the situation at the McCormick plant escalated into serious violence.

In *The Haymarket Tragedy*, historian Paul Avrich described the incident. People fired up by a speech delivered by anarchist leader August Spies walked to the picket lines to show solidarity with the fired workers and to heckle the scabs. The situation rapidly deteriorated; the Pickets attacked the replacement workers, forcing them back into the factory. Then the Pickets began throwing stones at the factory windows, breaking them. Police patrol wagons arrived at the scene. When the police moved into the crowd swinging billy clubs, the Pickets threw a hail of stones at the police. The police fired their revolvers into the crowd of Pickets, wounding many and killing two. The Pickets dispersed.

Anarchist labor leader August Spies witnessed the shootings. Infuriated, he returned to his organization's office and wrote and printed 2,500 copies of the following leaflet, of which about half were distributed:

REVENGE!

Workingmen, to Arms!!!

Your masters sent out their bloodhounds—the police—; they killed six of your brothers at McCormicks this afternoon. They killed the poor wretches, because they, like you, had the courage to disobey the supreme will of your bosses. They killed them, because they dared ask for the shortening of the hours of toil. They killed them to show you, "Free American Citizens!" that you must be satisfied and contended with whatever your bosses condescend to allow you, or you will get killed!

You have for years endured the most abject humiliations; you have for years suffered unmeasurable iniquities; you have worked yourself to death; you have endured the pangs of want and hunger; your Children you have sacrificed to the factory-lords—in short: You have been miserable and obedient slave all these years: Why? To satisfy the insatiable greed, to fill the coffers of your lazy thieving master? When you ask them now to lessen your burden, he sends his bloodhounds out to shoot you, kill you!

If you are men, if you are the sons of your grand sires, who have shed their blood to free you, then you will rise in your might, Hercules, and destroy the hideous monster that seeks to destroy you. To arms we call you, to arms!

Your Brothers[4]

While Spies was a radical, he was a very popular speaker among rank and file workers, so these angry, bitter sentiments may have struck a chord in many readers. Many workers felt that they were being exploited and that the government usually sided with the captains of industry during labor disputes. Willingness to use force was evident on both the part of management and labor.

A mass protest meeting was scheduled for the evening of May 4. Thousands of handbills were distributed stating, "Attention Working-men! Great Mass Meeting To-Night, at 7:30 o'clock, Haymarket, Randolph Street Bet Desplaines and Halsted. Good speakers will be present to denounce the latest atrocious act of the police, the shooting of our fellow-workmen yesterday afternoon."[5] In the first batch of handbills circulated, but deleted in the majority of the handbills, was the additional statement, "Workingmen Arm Yourselves and Appear in Full Force!"

Determined to avoid bloodshed, Chicago's mayor gave instructions to the superintendent of police to allow the meeting to proceed unless something should be said that would precipitate the kind of violence that occurred at the McCormick factory.

It was not a very large crowd that assembled at Haymarket Square that night; perhaps two or three thousand people. The speeches made were rather temperate, considering the violence at the McCormick factory. The hours moved on. Dark clouds threatening rain loomed overhead and the crowd dwindled to perhaps a tenth of its original size. It looked as if the meeting was ending peacefully when a nightmare scenario ensued. The last speaker uttered words that condemned the inequities in the law favoring capital against labor. When he urged his listeners to "kill the law," the police captain waiting nearby took this as sufficient reason to bust up the meeting. Marching his men quickly to the square, he ordered the people to disperse. Suddenly, without warning, a person unknown hurled a bomb into the ranks of the police. The bomb caused a large explosion that shattered windows for blocks around.[6]

After a moment of stunned silence, the police fired indiscriminately into the crowd. In the five minutes of slaughter that followed, the streets were filled with dead and wounded. The police alone sustained 67 casualties, many from shots fired from fellow officers in the darkness and confusion. The casualty count of civilians was almost certainly higher than that of the police inasmuch as the police were doing most of the shooting. The total number of civilian casualties is not known. In describing the reaction of the police, the *Chicago Tribune* observed that they seemed "goaded to madness," adding that "the police were in the condition of mind which permitted of no resistance, and in a measure they were as dangerous as any mob, for they were blinded by passion and unable to distinguish between the peaceful citizen and the Nihilist assassin."[7]

Public outcry against the anarchists was shrill. Newspapers all over the country cried out for reprisals. A Louisville newspaper suggested that the anarchists be "strung up." The Chicago police conducted a wide-reaching dragnet that trampled on Constitutional rights. Mail was intercepted. Homes were invaded without search warrants. Meetings were banned. Eventually, eight anarchists were arrested and tried. No credible evidence was ever produced that any of defendants had either thrown the bomb or participated in the bombing. Yet five of the men were convicted of a capital crime, largely on the basis of the judge's instructions to the jury. He said that if a person had advocated murder and another person was induced to commit murder by the first person's words, the first person was guilty of murder—even if the perpetrator could not be identified.

The question of whether the perpetrator even heard the words advocating violence was not considered relevant. Despite this novel and frightening construction of the law, the guilty sentences were upheld in the higher courts. The Supreme Court refused to hear the case. One of the five men committed suicide, the other four were executed.

In retrospect, the verdicts seem like a mockery of justice, but in a time of inflamed passions, justice is often the first casualty. The idea was to hang somebody; it didn't really matter very much who it was.

GREENWICH VILLAGE, NEW YORK CITY, 1969

Gays and lesbians have experienced more than their share of hostility from the larger society. Homosexual sex acts remain illegal in many places. Homosexuals have been the butt of jokes and caricatures and in some cases the victims of violent attacks now called "hate crimes." Many gays and lesbians kept their sexual activities secret rather than expose themselves to the hostile reactions of the larger society.

Among the bars that were heavily frequented by gays in New York City stood the Stonewall Inn, located on Christopher Street in Greenwich Village. In his book, *Stonewall,* Martin Duberman described the Inn as a hangout for male homosexuals rather than lesbians.[8] Formerly a straight restaurant and nightclub, it had been taken over by three Mafia figures and set up as a gay club. According to Duberman, the owners of the club paid about $2,000 a week to the local Sixth Precinct police for protection. When the owners were tipped off that a raid was expected, white warning lights would flash alerting the customers to forsake the dance floor and behave in an entirely prim and proper fashion. The system worked well; the owners made a handsome profit, gays had a place to socialize and the paid-off policemen smiled. It was corruption carried to the state of an art form.

Then one night the arrangement collapsed. At 1:20 A.M., the police marched into Stonewall unannounced. Unlike previous raids, there had been no prearranged tipoff. Still, the white lights flashed and the customers stopped touching and dancing. The police ordered the 200 customers who were inside to line up and present their I.D. cards. Then a paddy wagon arrived, parking on the street outside. As the police began to take people (employees of the Inn, a cross-dressed lesbian, drag queens) to the paddy wagon, the crowd turned sullen. Then the prisoners began to resist. A high heel of a drag queen thumped into the chest of a policeman and the prisoners fled the van with the police in hot pursuit. The crowd, now swelling, began to scream at the police. People threw coins, cans, bottles and bricks at the officers. The police were forced to retreat inside the bar. They drew their guns awaiting an onslaught.

Police reinforcements arrived, only to be greeted with jeers, rocks and bottles. By the time the police were able to clear the street, a number of people had been injured, some seriously, and the Stonewall Inn was in shambles.

The police raid and subsequent melee aroused strong feelings in many of New York's gays and lesbians. During the following day as evening approached, a crowd of several thousand people gathered in front of the Stonewall Inn. There was a carnival-like atmosphere with cheerleaders leading chants of "gay power." When the police tried to quell the demonstration, violence once again erupted. The police charged the crowd, swinging their nightsticks, and the people in the crowd threw bottles at the police.

During the following nights, the riots abated, picked up again, then ceased. While many of the more conservative members of the gay community were very unhappy with the rioters, the Stonewall incident sparked a wave of activism among homosexuals to redress long held grievances. The riot at Stonewall was considered a watershed in the gay rights movement.

LOS ANGELES—1965 AND 1992

Twilight was approaching on a waning summer day in South Central Los Angeles, an area called Watts. The year was 1965. Lyndon Johnson was in the White House, the Civil Rights revolution was in full swing. South Central Los Angeles seemed peaceful enough, on the surface. Yet, if one only scratched that surface, evidence of discontent would bubble up. Watts had become crowded. The population had swelled with African Americans migrating from all over the country in search of a better life. Housing was often substandard. In a third of the houses, plumbing was dilapidated or missing altogether.[9] Schools were overcrowded; many children were on half-day sessions. The jobless rate was twice that of the city as a whole. And the mostly-white Los Angeles Police Department was perceived by many residents as being not only hostile to blacks, but capable of acting brutally. The contrast of life in Watts with the glamorous images of other Los Angeles communities such as Hollywood was dramatic. Feelings of discrimination and relative deprivation were almost inevitable.

On that late summer day of 1965, an incident occurred that turned these pent-up feelings into an explosion of violence. In a searching photographic essay, "Understanding the Riots," the staff of the *Los Angeles Times* described this incident as a routine traffic stop, an event similar to incidents that happened thousands of times before and since. There was nothing that seemed special about what happened, yet the ripple caused by the event became a torrent. One thinks of chaos theory where small events can have profound consequences.

The incident happened at 116th Street and Avalon Boulevard. A highway patrolman had arrested a 21-year-old black woman on suspicion of drunk driving. A crowd gathered about the pair. Tempers flared. The policeman then arrested the suspect's brother and mother. Angry words and spitting gave way to throwing rocks and bottles. The police officer extricated himself and his suspects from the scene, but then all hell broke loose.

How this local, circumscribed incident turned into a riot that lasted six days, involving thousands of people is not clear, but soon people were chanting "Burn, baby, burn!" as stores were being looted and torched. The National Guard was called into action. When the riots were finally quelled and the residents of Watts looked at the ruins of a Safeway Store, the corner markets, the shoe stores, clothing stores, furniture stores and ballrooms, they could only then appreciate the extent of the devastation of their neighborhoods. Two hundred buildings had been destroyed and hundreds more had been damaged. The human toll included 34 deaths and more than 9,000 injuries. Nearly 4,000 people had been arrested.[10]

Many years elapsed between the Watts riot of 1965 and the riots that erupted following the acquittal of the policemen who savagely beat Rodney King in the spring of 1991. In the interim, civil rights legislation had all but wiped out legal discrimination against African Americans and affirmative action programs offered African Americans advantages in obtaining college education. Large numbers of African Americans had made major advances in the quality of their lives, holding good jobs and moving into suburban communities. In Los Angeles, a black man was now mayor. Still, there remained a large underclass living in the inner city. And still, there were reported incidents of police brutality. The ethnic composition of the area had changed appreciably. Many people from Asia had settled in the area and there was a large influx of people from Mexico. Entrepreneurs from Korea had opened stores in black neighborhoods, which led to racial conflicts between Koreans and blacks.

Unlike the riots of 1965 where the triggering event was a routine arrest witnessed by a few people, the triggering events for the 1991 riots were witnessed by the entire nation. The incident began on a March night after midnight. An African American, Rodney King, was driving with friends. They had been drinking. King, who was behind the wheel, passed a police car on the freeway. The police car flashed its red lights signaling King to pull over. Instead, he panicked and sped away. A chase ensued in which several police cars pursued King until he finally stopped near an apartment complex. Twenty-one police officers converged on the car. What happened next is in some dispute. The police said that they believed that King's actions indicated that he was dangerous, although witnesses contradicted this. Dangerous or not, several of the policemen began to brutally beat King. King was struck with metal batons 56 times and repeatedly kicked while on the ground. The blows shattered one of his eye sockets, fractured a cheekbone, and broke his leg.[11]

This incident of police brutality may have gone unnoticed in the larger scheme of things, except for the fact that a man with a video camera captured the scene on tape. These tapes were soon seen by people not only in Los Angeles but all over the nation.

The trial of the four police officers that were directly involved in the beating of Rodney King was moved from Los Angeles to the suburban community of Simi Valley. Somehow the defense team was able to persuade a jury to discount the violent acts in the video tapes and the testimony of the physicians who treated King following the beatings, and to accept the theory that the police felt threatened by King's behavior and that they were responding to this threat. How this theory squared with the repeated baton beatings and kicking the suspect when lying on the ground was difficult for many outside observers to understand, but so decided the jury.

The reaction to the King verdict was swift in coming. Violence erupted in South Los Angeles. Mobs dragged light-skinned motorists from their cars and beat them, sometimes brutally. Once again, revenge was exacted indiscriminately. The outnumbered police were unable to cope with the situation. It was mob rule. As night fell, looting and burning of buildings began. Trying to put out the growing number of fires, firefighters were met with rocks, bottles, and in some instances guns. One firefighter was shot in the cheek and suffered a stroke.[12]

The mayor instituted a dawn-to-dusk curfew. The National Guard was activated. The next day the riots continued. In the absence of sufficient police presence, looting was rampant. Some of the looters were in a festive mood, taking whatever they wanted. A stream of looters hauling booty out of the stores into waiting automobiles created a near gridlock. Chaos continued throughout the day. Both Korean and black store owners armed themselves to defend their property. At night, fires again lit up the sky.

As the riots continued into the week, the decision was made to send in 1,000 federal agents to help stop the violence. By the time sufficient force was mobilized to bring the situation under control, some parts of Los Angeles resembled a war zone. In "Understanding the Riots," the staff of the *Los Angeles Times* observed, "If one street defined the destruction, Vermont Avenue was it. It seemed to personify the city's broken spirit. For 10 miles between Santa Monica Boulevard in Hollywood and Manchester Boulevard in South Central Los Angeles, it had become a holocaust of fire-gutted buildings and shattered glass. Block after block, people's lives had been ripped apart."[13]

At least 45 deaths were attributed to the riots. The number of injuries was put at more than 2,000. It was estimated that 850 families were left homeless. Insurance losses were estimated at one billion dollars.[14]

Type II: Where the Privileged Feel Threatened

LOS ANGELES, OCTOBER 24, 1871

In his book, *Rioting in America*, Paul Gilje described several riots perpetuated by white Americans against Chinese immigrants.[15] The Chinese began coming to the western states in the 1840s. Immigration peaked in the 1870s, and then declined because of legal restrictions. The Chinese immigrants were probably best known for their work in building the western part of the railroad that spanned the continent.

To the dominant Anglos, the Chinese immigrants not only represented competition for jobs, they brought an alien culture the whites did not understand. That some Chinese ran opium dens or trafficked in prostitution served to create unflattering stereotypes about Chinese people and their culture.

The incident that triggered the October riot began with a gunfight between two rival Chinese gangs that had quarreled over a prostitute. An Anglo-American tried to interfere in the fight and was killed in the process. A policeman was also shot. The city's white population reacted to the shootings with fury. A mob moved into Chinatown, gutting the community. Houses were looted. Fifteen Chinese were hanged in this exercise of vigilantism.

This riot was not an isolated example. A few years earlier (February 1867) in San Francisco, a mob of several hundred whites attacked Chinese railway workers. Shanties and sheds were burned and a dozen Chinese workers were injured. The bloodiest disturbance occurred some years later in a coal mining camp at Rock Springs. A white mob sacked and looted a Chinese settlement, killing at least 51 Chinese Americans.

CICERO, ILLINOIS, JULY 1951

Compared to the riots in Los Angeles, the civil disturbance that happened in Cicero, Illinois in the summer of 1951 was small potatoes. Still, it shows the wrath that can be unleashed against people trying to make even a small dent in an established social order. My source for the Cicero riot is a report written at the time by retired attorney William Grant.[16] Grant noted that the events in Cicero received only scant notice in the New York newspapers, but became a *cause célèbre* in some foreign countries. During a trip to the Far East, then New York governor and twice presidential candidate Thomas Dewey found himself defending the United States against front page newspaper stories published in Singapore that described the Cicero riot.

The story began on June 10, 1951. A black family, the Clarks, tried to move some furniture into an apartment in Cicero that they had rented two days earlier. The Clarks were greeted by jeers and boos from on-looking white housewives. In addition to the outpouring of hostility from their prospective neighbors, the Clarks were approached by the police, who tried to persuade them to leave to prevent trouble. The Clarks responded to this pressure by filing suit against the officials of Cicero, claiming that they were part of a racial discrimination conspiracy. The judge issued a restraining order against the city and its officers, informing them that their responsibility was to get the Clarks peacefully settled into their apartment, not to get them out.

On a day in July shortly after the Clarks moved into the apartment, violence erupted. While onlookers cheered, teenagers tossed the Clarks' furniture out of their apartment onto the street. Then they set fire to the apartment. The riots initiated by this action lasted several days. The state police were called in and guardsmen set up barbed wire barricades to control what was called "a mob." State troopers remained in the community for two weeks. One hundred twenty-four people were arrested.

In this era in our history, before national civil rights legislation was enacted, the attempt by a black family to move into a white neighborhood could arouse extraordinary opposition. Many white people lived in segregated communities and were determined to keep them that way. In this segregated world, the attitudes of white people toward blacks were generally negative and often based on racial stereotypes. Blacks were seen as stupid and lazy and white people resisted having them as neighbors. In many cities, whites simply picked up and left, moving to the suburbs. It was an era of "white flight" with profound consequences for urban America. In Cicero, the reaction to the Clark family's move was one of intimidation followed by violence.

ATLANTA, SEPTEMBER 1906

Today's Atlanta is one of America's great cities. It enjoys the reputation of being dynamic and cosmopolitan and its leadership has included black mayors. It is hard to imagine how different Atlanta must have been in 1906 when it experienced terrible race riots. In newspaper articles of the time, blacks were referred to with such pejorative terms as "shiftless." Many white people were prepared to believe the worst about blacks.

Some accounts lay part of the blame for the Atlanta riots at the hands of the two leading gubernatorial candidates, who ran openly racist campaigns. These campaigns may well have poisoned the racial atmosphere. The trigger for the riots was stories published in "extra" editions of local newspapers claiming that black men had assaulted white women.

It was not clear that there was any truth to these stories, but it didn't really matter. Perception became reality. Interracial sexual contact was the ultimate transgression and when a man seized the moment, stood upon a box holding high the newspaper and asked the question whether Southern white men were going to stand for what happened, it was like firing on Fort Sumter all over again.

Shouts from the crowd of "No!" and "Kill the Negroes!" were followed by the formation of mobs—mostly young men and boys who took to the streets hunting down and beating up any blacks they came into contact with. The mob dragged two men from a trolley, killing them.[17] Two black barbers were taken from their barber shop while they were in the midst of shaving white customers. The barbers were shot to death and their bodies mutilated.[18] The mayor of Atlanta tried to stop the violence by appealing to the men to go home and let the law deal with the offenders. His appeal was ignored. When the mayor ordered a curfew, it was also ignored.

The mobs grew in size. A *New York Times* dispatch of September 24 reported that 10,000 white men and boys were in the mobs.[19] Blacks were demonized by participants as "black fiends." They were set upon, beaten, and in some instances, killed. At least ten blacks were killed and many more were injured.[20] As the riots grew in intensity, the black population of Atlanta melted into the countryside, taking their wounded and sometimes their dead with them for burial.

The governor of Georgia ordered the state militia to Atlanta to restore the peace. Arrests were made. The combination of the state militia, the flight of the black residents from Atlanta, and rainfall finally stemmed the riot but not before the mob took to smashing windows when its human targets had disappeared.

Solitary Heroes

Not everyone "loses it" when a riot begins. There are often unsung heroes; community leaders calling for calm, firefighters who risk their lives and individual citizens who act compassionately, sometimes heroically. In the 1992 riots in Los Angeles, white motorists brutalized by the black mob were saved by blacks. In a riot that occurred in Rosewood, Florida, in 1923, a white man hid black children from the rampages of a white mob. While others were infected by a virus of rage, these citizens remembered their humanity.[21]

The Role of the Police

Insufficient police presence can allow a developing riot to spread and become more intense. This was clearly the case in the 1992 Los Angeles riot where the number of police officers deployed were far too few to contain the violent reaction that followed the Simi Valley verdict in the Rodney King case. On the other hand, too great a police presence and overaggressive police tactics can turn a noisy but essentially peaceful gathering of citizens coming together to protest perceived injustices into a riot.

The history of the American labor movement records instances in which strikes were violently ended by law enforcement agents, state militia, and even federal troops. In the Haymarket Square tragedy the interventions of the police were unnecessary. While there was no excuse for the actions of the bomb thrower, the violence could well have been avoided.

Perhaps the most dramatic example of where over-aggressiveness by the police turned an admittedly difficult, tense situation into a bloody riot was what happened in Chicago during the Democratic Convention of 1968, 100 years after the Haymarket tragedy. In 1968 the Vietnam War was in full fury, bitterly dividing the American people. Thousands of war protestors came to Chicago to make their voices heard by the politicians nominating the Democratic presidential candidate. David Dellinger and Rene Davis, leaders of the main body of protestors, were committed to a peaceful, nonviolent demonstration. But when trouble erupted and a line of police officers waded into the crowd swinging batons, beating Davis to the ground in the process, many of the protestors were radicalized. All hell broke loose on the streets of Chicago.

The scene transmitted on network television horrified millions of Americans watching the convention and may well have cost Hubert Humphrey the presidency, altering American history in ways that can only be conjectured.

The Role of Propaganda and Inflammatory Writings and Speech

Anarchist August Spies could deliver a rousing speech. His rhetoric decrying the evils of capitalism had an impact on his audience of workers. On a fateful day in early May many of those who heard him talk became involved in the violence at the McCormick Reaper plant, which was the precursor to the tragedy at Haymarket Square. While Spies was not involved in the bombing at the Square, his rhetoric cost him his life. This travesty of justice aside, inflammatory rhetoric and hostile propaganda are not innocuous; the consequences of ugly words are sometimes ugly deeds.

Recall the incendiary newspaper headlines that precipitated the 1906 Atlanta riots. Once passions among young white males in Atlanta had been inflamed, a judicious inquiry into the truth of the allegations could not be made against blacks. A believing mob ruled.

During the 20th century there have been horrendous examples of propaganda used to promote violence. The Nazis elevated propaganda to an art form, using spectacles and the repetition of lies by a totally controlled media to help persuade the German people to accept the Nazi dogma that the Germans were a superior, master race and that their brutal actions, both within Germany and in other lands, were justified. The genocide in Rwanda was preceded by a propaganda barrage by the Hutu rulers and their allies in the media. Writing in the *American Psychologist*, David Smith observed that the Hutu leaders were "remarkably brazen in their propaganda." The Tutsis were accused of "the vilest crimes and designs, rarely with any hint of truthfulness.... What the radio said was coarse, violent, jocular, and full of anti–Tutsi demonology." Tutsis were said to be plotting the wholesale slaughter of Hutu innocents. Tutsi friends, neighbors, and even relatives were not to be trusted or tolerated; they were all, actually or potentially, traitors and mass murderers.[22] This propaganda helped pave the way for the murder of hundreds of thousands of people who happened to be different.

CHAPTER 9

Prevention and Treatment of Violent Behavior

S ome people are provoked very easily. They perceive misdeeds where none are intended. They react to minimal information, drawing swift conclusions of negative intent and acting on these conclusions. Sometimes these precipitous actions get people into trouble. Consider the young men who start fights thinking they have been disrespected. At times, as was the case of the unlucky Japanese exchange student who knocked on the door of a house in Louisiana asking for directions, rapid erroneous decision-making can lead to a fatal outcome.

The thresholds for feeling provoked and reacting are individual matters. Some people anger swiftly, others react in a more measured way. There is suggestive evidence that people with high, stable self-esteem are less swift to anger.[1] Feeling good about oneself over the years may make one less likely to take offense easily. If we could wave a magic wand and suddenly find ourselves in a nation of calm, confident people, our violent crime statistics might well plummet.

Unfortunately, our complex, high-energy society doesn't lend itself to quick, easy solutions for dealing with excessive anger and aggressiveness. We are not about to turn into Tahitians who have learned to live peacefully in an island paradise or Amish people who have turned their backs on the Industrial Revolution. Nor are we about to follow David Gil's prescription to radically alter our economic system.

The question becomes how can we raise the thresholds of overly aggressive individuals for feeling angry, and more importantly, for becoming aggressive and violent? How can we teach such people to hold their fire? The good news is that many people have worked hard on these issues and have come up with useful ideas. They have designed and evaluated programs to lower levels of anger, aggression and violence. Some of these programs focus on prevention, others on treatment. In this and the succeeding chapter, we shall explore some of these efforts.

Prevention vs. Treatment: Distinctions That Sometimes Blur

Prevention and treatment are usually viewed as two different concepts. In medicine we think of treatment when a physician tries to cure or ameliorate a disease that has been diagnosed by a pattern of symptoms or by laboratory tests. Prevention usually refers to efforts made to prevent the disease from occurring in the first place. Preventive health behavior includes such activities as exercising and eating a nutritious diet. Popular thinking has long recognized this distinction with such sayings as "An ounce of prevention is worth a pound of cure."

Efforts at prevention may be directed at an entire population such as spot announcements on the radio or television warning against the dangers of smoking. Efforts directed at an entire population, however, may not be cost-effective; it often makes more sense to target prevention efforts at groups within the population that are perceived to be at high risk. For example, anorexia and bulimia are disorders that occur principally in young women. It makes sense to concentrate preventive education about these disorders on teenage girls and young women, paying less attention to young men who have little risk of developing these disorders.

The distinction between prevention and treatment becomes blurred when we deal with people who have signs of a problem, but are not clearly diagnosed cases. The term "subclinical" is often used here. As an example, consider once again the eating disorder anorexia. A young girl may eat sparingly and exercise ferociously, trying to stay thin. Yet her weight may not fall within the guidelines allowing for a clinical diagnosis of anorexia. Her physician or parents might want to intervene at this point to try to prevent the development of anorexia. The regimen the girl may be put on (behavioral modification of her eating patterns, visits to a psychotherapist) may be similar to current treatment for anorexia.

A boy who is unruly and aggressive, but so far has not been suspended from school or picked up by the police for unlawful acts, presents a rough analogy to the teenage girl who looks like she could become an anorexic. The boy looks as if he is heading for trouble. If the decision is made to intervene in his life, the intervention may well take the form of trying to curb the boy's aggressiveness. To achieve this objective, the boy may be placed in a treatment program for aggressive children. So for this child, prevention and treatment become nearly undistinguishable.

Prevention Programs

Efforts to prevent violence run the gamut from the national level (e.g., legislation to put more police on the street, laws prohibiting the sale of firearms to convicted felons) to state and community programs (e.g., providing better street lighting, formation of neighborhood watch groups, providing recreation opportunities for teenagers) to the individual level (e.g., placing at-risk youngsters in programs teaching alternatives to violence).

On the national level, the Brady Law requiring background checks and waiting periods before the purchase of a handgun merits special attention. The Department of Justice reported that from March 1994 through the end of 1997, about 242,000 applications to buy handguns were denied as a result of the Brady Law. An analysis of 1997 data revealed that most of these denials (62 percent) occurred because the would-be purchaser was a convicted felon or was under indictment for a felony.[2] With the recidivism rate for criminals as high as it is, no one but the most die-hard opponent of gun control will be displeased by these statistics. It is impossible to say how many homicides were prevented by the Brady Law. The five-day waiting period alone has undoubtedly prevented some impulsive homicides and suicides. Time to cool off when one is angry and emotionally out of control can be a salutary preventive measure in itself.

The Brady Law was not an easy law to pass. The National Rifle Association fought the legislation vigorously and despite considerable public support for the measure, its enactment was a near thing. The experience of enacting gun control laws in Australia provides a sharp contrast to the tortuous process that occurred in America. A horrific incident that occurred on the Island of Tasmania just off of Australia's southern shore led Australians to act quickly and decisively. On a Sunday afternoon in April 1996, a lone gunman armed with assault rifles killed 35 people and injured 19 more. While fleeing the scene of the massacre in his car, he chanced upon a mother and her two young children. He shot the mother and her three-year-old daughter. Then, when the seven-year-old girl fled into the woods, he pursued her until he found her hiding behind a tree and killed her with his assault rifle.[3]

The reactions of the Australian populace was one of outrage. Shortly after the killings, legislation was introduced and passed banning the manufacture, sale and possession of all automatic and semi-automatic weapons. Gun registration was introduced and a 28-day waiting period was instituted between acquiring a gun permit and buying a gun.

Opinion polls indicated that 95 percent of the people supported the new gun laws.[4] The opposition of the Australian gun lobby proved ineffective. Australians had taken these murders personally.

In addition to these laws controlling firearms, the Australian government instituted a massive gun buy-back program offering fair market value for the newly banned guns. More than 640,000 guns were turned in by their owners.[5]

Community Violence Prevention Programs

In its publication *Reducing Youth Gun Violence*, the United States Department of Justice described a variety of programs that have been developed in communities around the nation that have the objective of preventing youth violence, and especially youth gun violence. Some of these programs are public education campaigns stressing the dangers of guns and the unacceptableness of using guns in settling disputes. Examples include the "Hands Without Guns" and the "Words Not Weapons" campaigns in Boston, Massachusetts and the "Youth Violence Prevention Network" in Fresno, California.[6] The Fresno program targeted at-risk Spanish speaking youth, using young people to communicate anti-gun violence messages. The program fostered gun-free zones in city parks and neighborhoods and employed mediation teams to work with high-risk youth. A noncommercial radio station, Radio Bilingue, played an important role in the effort, broadcasting both anti-violence messages and a special program called "Paz," that educated at-risk youth about the causes of violence and the effects of gun violence.

Graphic education about the effects of violence was provided by a program in Prince Georges County, Maryland, which borders on the nation's capital.[7] High school students were brought into the shock trauma and emergency rooms of the county hospital to watch physicians treating the wounds of the victims and perpetrators of violence. If this experience didn't bring home the dangers of firearms, it's hard to imagine what would.

Gun buy-back programs are another idea that has enjoyed some success, although nothing like the returns of the nationwide program carried out in Australia. Examples of community-based programs include the Prevention Partnership in Brooklyn, New York, which offered incentives for people to turn in guns for food vouchers, and Citizens for Safety, a program in Boston that enlisted the aid of neighborhood and youth organizations to remove more than 1,300 guns from circulation.[8]

A Role for the Media in Reducing Violence in the Community

Since most young people spend many hours each week watching television, a question that arises is, can the media play a role in reducing violence in the community? We already have seen evidence that exposure to television violence may increase aggressiveness.

What would happen if there were a coordinated media campaign in the community to reduce violence?

In Boston, Massachusetts, a mass media campaign was launched promoting an anti-violence message.[9] The campaign stressed such ideas as the risk of carrying guns, the tragic outcomes that can result from fights and the role that friends may play in escalating conflicts. The slogan used by the campaign was "Fighting is a lousy way to lose a friend. Friends don't let friends fight."

Thirty second spots were shown on television depicting a young person with a wounded friend. The spots highlighted the part the uninjured friend had played in escalating the conflict. In addition to the television spots, tee-shirts and posters inscribed with the campaign slogan were distributed in the neighborhoods.

Telephone surveys were conducted to find out how many people had seen the television spots and what impact the campaign had on attitudes toward violence. The results of the survey revealed that 42 percent of the teens contacted reported exposure to the media campaign. So a large number of young people were reached by the anti-violence message. Moreover, the teens who reported exposure to the message expressed attitudes that were more opposed to violence than the teens who said they had not been exposed to the message.

School-Based Anti-Violence Curriculums

Perhaps the most strategic place to teach attitudes opposed to violence and tactics to avoid escalating conflicts is the school. In today's increasingly crowded curriculum, violence prevention education is taking its place in many schools, along with education about drugs, AIDS, suicide, eating disorders and the other problems that confront today's generation of young people. Anti-violence curriculums are being developed, tried out in the schools, and in some cases, evaluated for effectiveness. A recent evaluation study was carried out by Alice Hausman and her colleagues assessing the effects of the "Violence Prevention Curriculum" developed by Deborah Prothrow-Stith.[10] The curriculum uses lectures, discussions and role playing exercises; the students meet for ten 40-minute sessions. The short course includes factual material about violence and teaches skills that can help a student prevent violence. Hausman's team compared the suspension rates of students taking the course with those of students in the same school not taking the course. The results were impressive. The students not taking the course were almost four times more likely to be suspended than the students taking the course.

Student Mediators

A school-based anti-violence program called the "Resolving Conflict Creatively Program" (RCCP) has been widely used in New York City, reaching 70,000 students in 180 schools. RCCP is taught by classroom teachers, beginning in the elementary schools and continuing through high school. An interesting feature of the program is the use of student mediators.[11] Students who are selected as mediators (this might be through peer nominations or a secret ballot) are given three days of intensive training. The students learn the skills of active listening, reflecting feelings, paraphrasing each disputant's position and asking questions to assist the parties in reaching a mutually acceptable solution to the problem. To be certified as a mediator, the candidates must demonstrate their skills in dealing with a role-played conflict.

Mediators work in pairs. In the elementary schools they wear tee-shirts fronted with the emblem "MEDIATOR" printed in bold letters. During lunch time and recess, they are on duty, keeping their eyes open for signs of trouble. When a conflict arises, the mediators approach the disputants, asking whether they want mediation. If the students agree (and this is usually the case) they retire to a quiet area and begin to talk.

In high school, the mediators act on referrals they receive from teachers and students. All mediators receive considerable ongoing coaching and supervision by the faculty coordinator, attending bi-weekly meetings to discuss their cases with the coordinator.

How well does student mediation work? A review of five schools during the school year 1988 to 1989 indicated that there was an average of 107 successful mediations per school.[12] If we can generalize these results to all of the New York City schools that used mediators, it would appear that hundreds if not thousands of conflicts were defused. Some of these conflicts would undoubtedly have led to violence. More than 80 percent of both teachers and students surveyed believed that students had been helped by the mediators. The mediators themselves reported that they had benefited from the experience.

While one could conjure up a host of unpleasant possibilities that could go wrong with such a program—after all, the children have a great deal of responsibility at an early age—if the program is carried out carefully and has wide support among the students, it looks as if it can be helpful in promoting a peaceful school environment.

Community Building

Research suggests that communities that are economically depressed, where the population is unstable and there is little formal or informal social organization tend to be prime areas for violent crime. When this is the case, we might expect that efforts to rebuild such communities, both socially and economically, would be accompanied by reductions in crime. In the United States today there are numerous examples of community based initiatives in which the residents of distressed communities have organized to improve their quality of life. In the monograph *Community Building Coming of Age*, C. Thomas Kingsley and his colleagues noted that by the year 1989, there were at least 2,000 local nonprofit Community Development Corporations (CDCs) in the United States.[13] While these groups have focused traditionally on developing better housing in their neighborhoods, some CDCs have engaged in community organization and developed programs for job training, family support and crime prevention.

An example of a comprehensive community development program was one undertaken in 1992 in the South Bronx of New York City. The CDCs have built new health facilities, developed employment and training programs, established partnerships with local schools to improve the quality of education, initiated crime reduction measures, and were involved in economic development including the construction of a new shopping center.[14]

To assess the effects of such CDC initiatives on the reduction of violent crime, it would be instructive to compare "before and after" crime statistics in these communities with comparable communities that did not have active CDC programs.

Kingsley and his colleagues described a community program that had as its major focus crime reduction. The community, the Boyd-Booth neighborhood in Southwest Baltimore, was experiencing serious problems brought on by an open-air drug market.[15] A newspaper story reported that the residents heard gunshots at night and saw blood on the streets in the morning. People retreated into their homes, unwilling to report the drug dealing activity to the police, because they feared retaliation from the dealers. The article stated that the people who could leave the neighborhood had left.

After the newspaper story appeared, community leaders decided to take action. They instituted a program to attack the drug trade. With the cooperation of the police and other city and non-governmental agencies, they began to deny drug dealers the space to carry out their transactions. They boarded up abandoned buildings and fenced off alleys. They met with the local landlords to secure their cooperation and held community marches to get more people involved. To drive the message home that they were taking back their community, they held picnics and cookouts on the very street corners that were used to sell drugs. Finally, the community leaders provided summer youth programs and special activities for the young people of the neighborhood to offer positive alternatives to drug dealing. During a two-year period drug arrests in the community decreased by 80 percent and violent crime decreased by 52 percent.[16]

Sometimes, even making one or two critical changes in a community can make a difference in the level of crime. In an inner city neighborhood in San Antonio, Texas, a group of citizens gathered evidence about a convenience store that was selling alcohol to underage buyers and selling drugs. The citizens kept count of the number of young people who purchased alcoholic beverages, then successfully petitioned the local Alcohol and Beverage Commission to close the store. The crime rate in the community dropped significantly.[17]

Community involvement is thought to be crucial in reclaiming a neighborhood. Social scientists who have studied this problem stress that in order to have lasting change, the people who live in the neighborhood must be participants in making the changes and seeing that they stick.

The new emphasis on community policing can mesh well with

these citizen efforts. When the individual police officer becomes known to and trusted by the citizens, this can increase cooperation in fighting and preventing crime. Police officers who visit schools in the community, attend community meetings, talk to the citizens and are visible on the street can in time have a perceptible impact on crime prevention in the community.

Programs for At-Risk Children

The case for intervention with children who show signs of developing conduct disorders was made succinctly by John Lochman and his colleagues. They pointed out that early intervention may interrupt the child's movement into a pattern of conduct disorders (aggression and delinquency) before such patterns "become broad, overlearned and automatic and before years of peer and adult counteraggression and rejection have accumulated," hardening these behaviors.[18] The logic of this position seems unassailable. Turn a child around early and you may not only help him to a better life, you may prevent him from injuring or killing someone else in future years. While the idea is laudable, there are difficulties involved in carrying it out.

The first step in developing an intervention program is to accurately identify children who are at risk for future violent and delinquent behaviors. Research has identified some broad indicators for such future troubles as a family history of violence, an aversive child rearing environment and especially early aggressive behavior by the child. Reliable instruments are now available for assessing aggressive behavior in young children. These instruments, which utilize ratings of children's behavior made by their teachers and parents, seem like reasonable candidates for screening devices.

Lochman and his colleagues administered such rating forms to the teachers and parents of 382 kindergarten students. Then, they waited a year and a half to see how these children behaved in the first grade. The researchers were particularly interested in whether the child showed signs of externalizing behavior problems. Seventy percent of the children categorized as "high risk" by the screening instruments administered during kindergarten showed problem behaviors during the first grade, compared to 21 percent of those categorized as low risk. At first blush, these results look impressive. The predictive value of the screening instruments were well above chance. Still, if the screening tests were used to assign at-risk children to intervention programs, large numbers of erroneous placements would be made. As the authors pointed out, "Approximately 30 percent of the children identified in this study as at being high risk were false positive.... The major concerns for the false-positive children are that they may be stigmatized in some way by being classified as high risk and that they might suffer iatrogenic effects because of their involvement in the intervention."[19]

So, one has to be concerned about inadvertent negative effects that would not have happened if the children were left alone.

That's not all the bad news. The authors went on to state that "In this study, nearly 50 percent of the children who ultimately displayed problem outcomes in the first grade were false negative.... The concern for these children is that they would not have received services although they ultimately appear to have been in need of service."[20]

For a medical test, such as identifying women with uterine cancer, an error rate of this magnitude would be catastrophic. For identifying children who need help to prevent conduct problems, the error rate is less troublesome, but still too high to be comfortable. It is possible that the inclusion of other measures in the screening battery could improve the predictability of the instrument. The goal of developing a screening battery for young children that has more acceptable levels of accuracy is an important one and should be a high priority for researchers.

Working with Aggressive Children

It is important to remember that while many children who are aggressive at early ages will become involved in delinquency when they are adolescents, a significant number of young aggressive children will cease aggressive acts without participating in any formal program of therapy or behavior modification. Studies suggest that decreases in aggressive behavior often take place during the transition from preschool to elementary school and in late adolescence.[21] These spontaneous changes underscore the need for control groups in research that studies the effectiveness of intervention programs.

In the absence of highly accurate screening instruments, it is difficult to know which children should be selected for programs to decrease aggressive behavior and which children should be left alone. Children who persist with aggressive, unruly and disruptive behavior past the initial years of elementary school are probably good candidates to consider for intervention. The decision to place a child in a program for aggressive children should be made cooperatively by the child's parents, teachers and the school psychologist.

Social Skills Training for Aggressive Children

It has been observed that many children who are unusually aggressive have poor social skills; they simply are not very good at relating to other children.[22] If such children are placed in a training program to improve their peer coping skills, would their levels of aggressiveness decrease? An interesting study carried out by Ronald Prinz and his colleagues suggests this may be the case.[23]

The researchers selected two types of children for their training program: aggressive children and children who were socially competent but not aggressive. Four aggressive and four nonaggressive children were placed in groups that met at school under the guidance of trained adult leaders. The meetings of the groups were not spontaneous, free-wheeling affairs. Rather, the activities were structured. During one part of the meeting, the children took turns relating things that happened to them since the last meeting. In another part of the meeting, the students interacted on a one-on-one basis in which an aggressive child was paired with a competent nonaggressive child. The adult leader instructed one of the two children to disclose things about himself, such as what made him feel happy during the week. The adult leader also instructed the child to ask the other child questions such as what did he really do well during the week. The leader listened and observed, evaluating the aggressive child's conversational skills. If the child did not do well, the leader worked with him until he improved.

The training program also involved some group activities. Evaluation of the program revealed that in comparison to a control group of children who did not receive the training, the children who took the training showed a significant reduction in teacher-rated aggression. There were no adverse effects reported for the competent, nonaggressive children who participated.

Consider another approach to teaching social skills—this time for adolescents, rather than young children. The assumption underlying the approach was that teaching at-risk youth how to interact more constructively with their peers—to solve problems and resolve conflicts using non-violent strategies—would reduce the propensity for violent acts. The program, designed by W. Rodney Hammond and Betty Yung, was tailored specifically for African American youth.[24]

The students chosen for the program were typically 12 to 15 years old and included both boys and girls. Some of the students had evidenced little in the way of social skills, others had a history of behavior problems or had been victims of aggression. The training took place in school, in groups of 10 to 12 students. The students were given either 37 or 38 training sessions lasting about 50 minutes each.

The students were shown videotaped vignettes portraying various social skills such as giving positive feedback, giving negative feedback, accepting negative feedback, resisting peer pressure, solving problems and negotiation. The tapes began by dramatizing a conflict that might escalate into a violent confrontation. As this point approached in the drama, the narrator froze the action and described a skill that could have been used by one of the parties to prevent the escalation of the conflict. Then, the drama was replayed on the tape—this time with one of the actors using this skill, showing how the conflict could be dealt with without violence.

In their training sessions, the students role played such situations themselves. Their role playing efforts were videotaped so that the students could become more aware of their own actions.

An evaluation of the training compared 15 students who completed the training with a comparable group of 13 students who were untrained. None of the trained students were suspended or expelled from school because of violence. In the control group, there were two expulsions, six in-school suspensions, and one out-of-school suspension. Although the sample sizes used in the evaluation were obviously small, the results were clearly promising.

Treating Violent Adolescents

It is one thing to talk about reducing aggressiveness in at-risk school children; it is another to talk about changing behavior of adolescents who have been incarcerated for violent crimes. In a review of the admittedly limited research on this problem, David Tate and his colleagues noted that traditional psychotherapy emphasizing insight and relationships has not proven particularly effective with violent adolescents.[25] Nor has group therapy. There is some evidence that social skills training may be beneficial for these offenders, although the jury is still out on long-range benefits. Here are two examples of such programs.

A program with the acronym ART (Aggression Replacement Training) taught incarcerated adolescents a broad range of pro-social skills as well as anger control and moral reasoning. The researchers reported that the adolescents who received the training behaved more constructively while they were within the correctional institution.[26] The second program called the Viewpoints Training Program sought to change adolescents' views about the legitimacy of violence and to teach them social problem-solving skills. In an evaluation study, adolescents incarcerated for violent crimes attended 12 sessions of workshops on social problem solving. They improved their problem-solving skills and were rated by the staff as less aggressive and impulsive than adolescent offenders not given the training. The adolescents who participated in the training showed positive changes while they were within the institution, but they did not have fewer parole violations during the 24 months following their release.[27]

It may be that psychologically-oriented programs focused on change in behavior or attitudes will have only a limited reach on violent offenders when they return to their old environments. More comprehensive efforts involving the person's family, friends and community may be required to give these psychological changes produced in the prison program a chance to take root.

Multisystemic Therapy (MST), developed by Scott Henggler and Charles Borduin and their colleagues, is such an approach.[28] MST does not focus exclusively on the individual adolescent. Rather, interventions are also directed at the multiple problem areas within the youth's environment. The rationale underlying MST is that young people function within interconnected social environments that encompass individual, family and extrafamilial (school, peers, neighborhood) factors. MST assumes that behavior problems can be triggered by negative events that happen within any one or a combination of these environments. Interactions should be directed to wherever the problems appear, and this may involve multiple efforts.

In practice, therapists trained in the procedures usually meet with the youth's families in their homes. The meetings might last as much as 90 minutes, but typically are shorter. In one study of the technique, families were seen on the average for about 13 weeks.

Evaluation of multisystemic therapy suggests that this approach can be effective. A study was carried out on 84 juvenile offenders, the majority of which had been arrested at least once for violent crimes such as assault and battery with intent to kill.[29] Half of these offenders were given multisystems therapy; the other half were given the usual services for offenders. At 59 weeks following referral, youths who received the multisystemic therapy were about half as likely to be rearrested as those who received the usual services. The families that received multisystemic therapy seemed more cohesive and the young people receiving therapy were less aggressive with their peers. The results of this study showed that MST is a promising approach. A comprehensive program may be the best hope for preventing violent offenders from repeating their crimes.

CHAPTER 10

Strategies for Anger Control: A View from the Therapist's Office

When a person begins to feel angry and the anger begins to mount like a crescendo in Tchaikovsky's *1812* Overture, wouldn't it be nice if an alarm signal went off in the person's mind flashing a "stop" sign before he or she begins firing the cannons, as they sometimes do during the climax of the overture. If somehow he or she could stop, pause and consider before using those angry words, or worse, throwing those punches.

The signal that one's anger is rising, getting out of control, almost has to come from within. There may be no friend or family member who can be counted on to raise that yellow flag to warn you that "You're losing it" and to "Cool it before you do something you'll regret." A person who might raise such warnings, even in the most diplomatic way, may feel that he or she is all too likely to become the target of the swelling anger and feel reluctant to tempt fate by intervening.

The signal that comes from within to warn that anger is rising toward the danger point is a combination of physiological arousal and hostile thoughts. Physiological arousal is that often-discussed fight-or-flight reaction that served our ancestors well when they faced down dangerous animals with spears tipped with stone points. While the mobilization reaction may serve us less well now in the intricacies of modern life, the physiology involved is probably similar. When your mood and thought processes are overwhelmed with storm clouds, try feeling your pulse. It's probably running faster than usual.

Sometime—when you're about to launch into a heated argument—excuse yourself before you unload that salvo and venture into another room where there is a mirror. Take a good look at your face. Is that the face of a thoughtful, rational individual or do you look put out, grim and angry? If you think of yourself as a sensible sort of person, you might want to shake your head at the mirror image, step back and ask, "What is going on?" You might even venture a smile and suggest to yourself, surely there must be a better way.

Let's examine some possibilities that have been developed by therapists working in clinical settings for dealing with angry feelings. Some of these approaches have applicability in everyday life, although they would require some working sessions with a trained therapist to put them into practice.

Fair Fighting

There is a school of thought in psychology that espouses the view that expression of negative feelings, including anger, is healthy in an interpersonal relationship. The idea has some obvious attractions. Keeping one's feelings perpetually bottled up is neither healthy for oneself nor a relationship that may suffer from the cumulative buildup of resentments. Ultimately, there may only come an explosion—another manifestation of that tightly coiled spring we alluded to when discussing drinking and violence. However, this need for ventilation has to be balanced against the negative consequences of being accusative and worse, demeaning in verbal exchanges in a relationship. The data from Baumeister's study is unequivocal in pointing to the damage such remarks may inflict in a relationship. Harsh words unsaid can be the best things that never happened.

The "let's fight it out" school of thinking may have had its heyday in the late 1960s when therapists led by George Bach developed a fight training treatment program.[1] The therapists working at the Institute of Group Psychotherapy in Beverly Hills, California (which may say something about the generalizeability of the approach) encouraged couples to verbally fight to air their negative feelings. The idea was not simply to fight, but to fight fair. The individuals were not supposed to scapegoat each other or snipe at each other destructively. The therapists even developed a fight-scoring system to see how the fight affected the relationship.

It has been my opinion for many years that if the two people involved were both comfortable with fighting as a way of life, were thick-skinned and got over hurt feelings easily, the fair-fight routine might be a workable approach. What happens, though, if one party tends to get upset by fights and starts to catalog hurts and resentments? The relationship may soon be dead in the water. Fair fighting, or for that matter, any kind of fighting on a regular basis, is a high risk strategy for a relationship.

Ventilation of angry feelings, then, has its positives and negatives, with a considerable risk of unintended, unhappy consequences. Perhaps the ultimate exercise in ventilating angry feelings was the fictional account rendered in George Orwell's chilling novel *1984*. Every day, for two minutes, members of the "ruling party" participated in what was called the "hate." The assembled party members watched on a tele-screen a speech by the nation's arch-enemy and were expected to react to his words with fury. The viewers shouted, gesticulated and threw objects at the screen in what amount to a daily grand catharsis.[2]

Some Techniques from Behavioral and Cognitive Therapies

Here are some additional approaches that therapists have developed to help patients better cope with their angry feelings. These methods have been shown to be effective in evaluation studies.[3] Initial training with a therapist is probably essential. The first method includes the pairing of a relaxation response with imagery of situations that normally elicit an aggressive response. Initially, the subject is taught the technique of deep muscle relaxation. The skill is usually easily learned after a few sessions of instruction and when practiced can leave one feeling very relaxed, almost limp. In this deeply relaxed state the subject is asked to imagine scenes that tend to provoke angry reactions. The therapist begins with a scene that is only mildly provocative. If imagining this scene does not cause more than a ripple in the subject's relaxed state, the therapist proceeds to a slightly more disturbing scene. As long as the subject does not react unduly, the procedure continues, allowing the subject to think about—or better, visualize—a gradually escalating series of scenes that would normally elicit an angry response. Pairing these imagined scenes with deep muscle relaxation usually allows the subject to tolerate these scenes without getting as upset as he or she normally would.

A second approach to dealing with anger-provoking situations is based on the principles of cognitive therapy.[4] Perceptions and beliefs often give rise to angry reactions. Perceived misdeeds are typically cited by people as the reasons for their angry feelings. If there is not an adage that "There is more than one way to look at an event," there should be, and this includes the actions of others that are perceived as misdeeds. One could interpret the action of another person as an intentional effort to hurt or injure, or one could interpret it as an accident, an oversight, a failure of communication or the result of an understandable set of circumstances that was not hostile in intent. Looking at an event through one of these prisms makes the action seem less of a misdeed and thus easier to forgive and forget. Training people to examine alternative possibilities and not to automatically assume the worst possible case can reduce the likelihood of an angry response.

Are all perceived misdeeds simply innocuous actions? Of course not. But a great many may turn out to be less than meets the eye.

Cooling Off Periods

Most of the approaches we are discussing in this chapter are inventions of psychotherapists. Cooling off periods are not. This is a common-sense approach with much to recommend it. Consider a family conflict in which a father and son are at loggerheads about the son's behavior and are about to exchange harsh, angry words. Before this happens, wouldn't it be a good time to put some space and time between the would-be combatants so that they have time to reflect? Space and time may allow angry feelings to subside and positive feelings to reassert themselves, affording an opportunity for the parties to find effective ways to deal with the issues that have divided them. The beauty of a cooling off period is that it gives both parties a chance to step back and consider. Cooling off periods have been long used in settling labor disputes and are a tactic employed by mediators in resolving school conflicts.

Taking the Other Person's Perspective

When it is important to preserve a relationship, emphasis should be put on resolving conflicts in ways that are mutually acceptable. In order to practice such "win-win" conflict resolution, it is helpful, and often essential, to have a thorough understanding of the issues that are troubling the other party. It is difficult to obtain such an appreciation of another person's thoughts and feelings by simply arguing for your own point of view or offering unsolicited advice. What is necessary to do is to listen, and listen well.

A therapist learns such skills early in the game. If not, he or she may soon be out of business. For above all else, many patients seek someone who will listen to them and make an effort to understand what is bothering them. This is a key component of the therapeutic relationship.

We are not advocating the idea that in everyday interactions a person should attempt to play-act the part of a therapist. But almost all of us can listen more attentively and try to understand better. We can also advance a step beyond attentive listening and ask the question, "What would it be like to see the world through the eyes of another person?" This is not an easy thing to do, but it can be instructive. His or her perspective, values, beliefs differ from your own. If you can glimpse what the realities seem like to the other party, you are in a better position to accommodate his or her needs in decisions that affect you both.

We use the word "empathy" to describe the ability to feel what another person is feeling. It is reading another person's moods and understanding what he or she is experiencing. Psychologists have suspected that people who have these abilities are less likely to be aggressive. It may be that the empathic person is sensitive to the negative reactions that aggressive acts engender in others and may conclude that it is a price they do not wish to pay themselves. They may have concluded that aggression is generally counterproductive or it may simply be that sympathetic understanding and chronic aggression tend to be antithetical personality traits.

A meta-analysis of research studies has confirmed the hypothesis that empathy and aggressiveness are negatively related; people who are aggressive tend to score lower on questionnaire measures of empathy.[5]

Problem Solving

Conflict resolution is an effort to resolve problems that occur in human relationships. In romantic relationships, family relationships and situations in the workplace, problems can arise ranging from the trivial (what television program to turn on) to the significant (e.g., whether to relocate to another city). In labeling certain problems trivial, we are not underestimating their impact. On the contrary, a series of minor hassles can lead to explosions, or be associated with the development of depressive reactions.[6]

Perhaps the optimum time to confront problems is when they are still in an emergent state, before they begin to elicit feelings of anger and lead to smoldering resentments. Ideally, the plan would be for the people involved to sit down together in an atmosphere that is not emotionally charged, where there is a relatively low level of defensiveness and the participants are not frozen in their positions. The goal is to generate solutions (or a package of solutions) to the problem in which everyone involved comes out with some positive outcome—a win-win solution. A winner-take-all outcome is not likely to be a healthy one for people who want to build viable relationships.

The processes involved in problem-solving can be formalized, but generally they include brainstorming, negotiation and commitment. Brainstorming is a free-wheeling, open-ended process that has the objective of getting as many ideas as possible on the table for discussion. Everyone present is encouraged to offer ideas. In order not to discourage the free flow of ideas, criticisms of the ideas in the initial stage of brainstorming should be withheld or at least muted. As the process proceeds, ideas can be critically analyzed, modified, combined or deleted if they are deemed unwise or not feasible.

Negotiation involves taking the ideas that survive scrutiny and putting them in some kind of package involving mutual obligations. "I will do this, you will do that." Issues of when, where and how much are discussed and agreed upon. At the end of the process, all parties should feel comfortable enough with the agreement to verbally commit to carrying out its terms.

Only time and experience will reveal whether the agreement is workable and produces satisfying results. If it does not, the parties revisit and try again, applying the insights gained in the interim to achieve a better result.

Attributions for Failures and Mistakes

Everyone makes mistakes. Almost everyone suffers reversals. When this happens, it is part of our human condition to look for explanations. Blaming others is a route many people follow. It is easier to look for cause in the misdeeds of others than to look within. A worst case example of this occurred in the 1920s and 1930s when Adolph Hitler persuaded many Germans that Germany lost the First World War because of the Jews. These anti–Semitic diatribes were first steps on the way to the Holocaust.

To look within for mistakes is harder to do than to cast one's net about searching for scapegoats. Looking within, however, offers the possibility of making constructive changes. The proposition is simple. If you know what you are doing wrong, you might be able to do it better. In this kind of introspective analysis, it is all-important that the individual does not get too hard on himself or herself. Becoming angry with oneself can be depressogenic. The trick is to acknowledge that no one is perfect, that we all make mistakes, and then ask, "What can I learn from my errors?"

The perfectionist who cannot tolerate errors in either himself or others travels a difficult road in life; the perfectionist is both vulnerable to depression and can make other people miserable.[7] If a person can't take a charitable view of his own errors, looking within may be counterproductive.

A politician was said to have remarked, "Don't get mad—get even." What I am advocating is, "Don't get mad—get smart." If others are clearly causing the problem—try to convene a forum for problem solving to deal with the issues. If one's own behavior is the problem, find a different way to behave.

Behavioral Changes

Frustration is often involved in the chain of events that leads to aggressive reactions. In the "get smart—not angry" approach, it makes sense to reduce chronic frustrations. To some extent, this takes us back to problem solving—alone or with others, searching for alternative ways of doing what you are currently doing. It may be finding a different time to shop in order to avoid the crowds in the stores or paying your bills electronically to lighten the nuisance of paperwork. In addition to making alterations in what you are doing to make things run more smoothly, consider adding activities into your life that are personally gratifying. These may be activities that you used to do and enjoyed, but fell by the wayside under the press of job and family life. I have had patients who had to give up too much of what was important to them when they found themselves in the juggernaut of having a career, running a home and raising children. Deleting these once valued activities proved to be a source of resentment as well as a loss of outlets that were needed to maintain an emotional equilibrium. For my patients, "making time" to reinstitute these activities proved beneficial. There may also be activities that you have always fancied yourself doing—but never quite got around to. Learning to play golf, taking a trip to a foreign shore, writing, painting, learning to play a musical instrument—whatever it may be, at long last, why not do it? You may never become another Jack Nicklaus, Ernest Hemingway or Pablo Picasso, but so what? If it turns out that you enjoy it, your life will be richer and you may experience more of what Maslow called self-actualization.

We have outlined some potentially useful ways for dealing with anger. In closing this chapter, we would like to call attention to a way of dealing with anger that many of us engage in that is likely to be ineffective and counterproductive. This is ruminating about one's angry thoughts and concurrently reexperiencing one's anger. One may draw an analogy here with depressed feelings. The person who is feeling depressed and who self-focuses tends to get worse, not better. The depressed mood is simply deepened by going over and over the problem, which is usually formulated by the person in the worst possible light. Distraction can be a saving grace for people prone to this destructive type of thinking.[8]

In regard to anger, ruminating about perceived misdeeds does not make the incidents disappear. Using a cognitive therapy approach, one might try to reframe the incidents to make them more palatable and less egregious, but simply going over the situation on one's mind, again and again, will probably only make one feel angrier. It is difficult to turn off anger like a faucet, but replaying grievances in one's mind is only likely to exacerbate the problem. A series of experiments carried out by Cheryl Rusting and Susan Nolen-Hoeksema supports this clinical observation and suggests that as is true for depressed mood, distraction may be of some help in turning off the stream of personal grievances.[9]

Notes

Introduction

1. Buss & Shackelford (1997), p. 605.
2. Trinkaus & Shipman (1994), p. 340.
3. Whitman (1995).

Chapter 1

1. Alberts (1994), p. 16.
2. Aristotle (1913), p. 808. The quotation was cited in Russell (1994), p. 102.
3. See for example Ekman (1993) and (1994) and Izard (1980). For a critical review of this work see Russell (1994).
4. Boucher & Carlson (1980).
5. Ekman (1993), p. 389.
6. Sharkin (1988), p. 361.
7. Rubin (1986), p. 116.
8. Novaco (1994), p. 321.
9. Speilberger, et al. (1983), p. 16.
10. Rubin (1986), p. 116.
11. Ibid., p. 116.
12. Russell & Fehr (1994). See Table 3, p. 192. In a previous investigation the researchers applied the techniques to the concept of love. See Fehr & Russell (1991).
13. Averill (1983).
14. Ibid., p. 1150.
15. See, for example, Beck (1976) and Wickless & Kirsch (1988).

16. Fitness & Fletcher (1993), p. 945.

17. Ibid., p. 945.

18. The diary technique was first described in Robbins, Meyersburg and Tanck (1974). In our first study, students were asked to fill out the diary for one week.

19. Robbins & Tanck (1997), p. 495.

20. Ibid.

21. These examples were taken from our raw data. There are many similar examples in the data.

22. Robbins & Tanck (1997).

23. Ibid., p. 495. Some of the examples used were taken from the article. Others were selected from our raw data.

24. Wickless & Kirsch (1988), p. 376.

25. Herodotus (1942), pp. 511–512.

26. Averill (1983), p. 1146.

27. Robbins & Tanck (1997), p. 492.

28. Nowlis & Green's Adjective Check List (1963) was the first instrument of this type that I am aware of. Other researchers (e.g., Zuckerman & Lubin, 1965) have also developed adjective check lists.

29. Spielberger & Sydeman (1994). Test-retest correlations for state anger were in the .2 range. See p. 303.

30. Ibid. Test-retest correlations for trait anger were in the .7 range. See p. 303.

31. Novaco (1975).

32. Novaco (1994), p. 329.

33. The list of coping techniques was presented in Robbins & Tanck (1978) and (1992). Some of the analyses presented here (e.g., the perception of the effectiveness of different coping techniques) have not been previously reported.

34. The original factor analysis was presented in Robbins, et al. (1974). See p. 580.

Chapter 2

1. Robbins & Tanck (1997).

2. Averill (1983), p. 1147.

3. Mikolic, et al. (1997).

4. Pan (1997).

5. Keister (1984).

6. Bredemeier & Shields (1985).

7. Feinstein (1996). See p. 379.

8. Steinbeck (1962), p. 52.

9. For a discussion of instrumental aggression, see Cornell, et al., (1996).

10. Ibid.

11. Pepler, et al. (1998).

12. See Buss & Durkee (1957) and Buss & Perry (1992).

13. See Buss (1961).

14. Calvert & Tan (1994).

15. Berkowitz (1983), p. 1135.

16. Shakespeare (1938), p. 186.

17. For a review of the research relating temperature and aggression, see Anderson (1989) and Anderson & Bushman (1998).

18. Anderson (1989), p. 93.

19. Reported on radio station WTOP, Washington D.C., March 2, 1997.

20. Dollard, et al. (1939). For a more contemporary perspective on the frustration-aggression hypothesis, see Berkowitz (1989).

21. See Bredemeier & Shields (1985). The story was attributed to Melvin Mark of Pennsylvania State University and his colleagues.

22. DiLalla & Gottesman (1991).

23. Ibid., p. 126.

24. Cloninger, et al. (1982).

25. DiLalla & Gottesman (1991), p. 126.

26. See Miles & Carey (1997). The authors noted that the influence of heredity on aggression was less clear when observational measures were used rather than self-reports or parental reports.

27. See for example Hay (1984).

28. Buss & Perry (1992).

29. Bettencourt & Miller (1996).

30. Mikolic, et al. (1997).

31. Magdol, et al. (1997).

32. Ibid. These data are presented in Table 1, p. 71.

33. Ibid., p. 75.

34. Ibid., p. 76.

35. Crick & Bigbee (1998).

36. See Harris, et al. (1996), p. 321.

37. Dabbs & Morris (1990).

38. See for example Harris, et al. (1996).

39. For a review of studies linking testosterone and athletic competition, see Gladue, et al. (1989).

40. Ibid.

41. Harris, et al. (1996).

42. Gladue (1991).

43. Van Goozen, et al. (1994). Van Goozen, et al. (1995).

44. Gladue and Bailey (1995) reported that heterosexual males were more physically aggressive than homosexual males. In a 1991 study, Gladue found no difference in this regard. In the 1991 study, Gladue found that heterosexual women were more physically aggressive than homosexual women, but this was not replicated in the 1995 study.

45. For a review of studies relating serotonin and aggressiveness, see Berman, et al. (1997).

46. Coccaro & Kavoussi (1997).

Chapter 3

1. Scherer, et al. (1988). See also Mesquita & Frijda (1992) for related papers.

2. Borke & Su (1972).

3. Schieffelin (1983), p. 186.

4. Rosaldo (1980).

5. Chagnon (1983).

6. Ibid., p. 171.

7. Bonta (1997), p. 300.

8. Endicott (1988). For abstracts describing the Batek people as well as the other peoples cited in Bonta's article, see Bonta pp. 317–320.

9. Overing (1986).

10. Levy (1973).

11. Munch (1945).

12. Norberg-Hodge (1991).

13. See Bonta, p. 302 for a discussion of the education of Amish children.

14. Department of Justice Statistics reveal a very large disparity (a ratio over 5 to 1) between families with incomes under $9,999 and families with incomes over $30,000 for reports of violence toward women attributable to an intimate. See *Violence Between Intimates* (1994).

15. Kupersmidt, et al. (1995).

16. Bonta (1997), p. 313.

17. Ibid., p. 301.

18. Ibid., p. 308.

19. Kraybill (1989).

20. Tuchman (1988), p. 36. Tuchman's statement was made in a discussion of the 16th century religious conflicts in the Netherlands.

21. The circumflex model of personality following the early work of Timothy Leary uses a circle with north and south points labeled dominant and submissive behaviors and east and west points labeled affiliative (friendly) and oppositional behaviors. The part of this circle lying between dominant and oppositional points is aggressive behavior. See Leary (1957). On a macro level, the desire of some states to impose their will over other states—to exercise domination is a very old story. Thucydides related a dialogue held during the Peloponnesian War (circa 416 B.C.) in which the Athenians, about to attack and conquer the small island of Melos, reacted to the protests of Melian emissaries that such conquest was unwarranted and unjust by stating that "right, as the world goes is only in question between

equals in power, while the strong do what they can and the weak suffer what they must." Here was an early exercise in real-politik. See Thucydides (1934), p. 331.

22. See Shreeve (1995), p. 295.

23. Ibid., pp. 296–297

24. Hochschild (1998).

25. Ibid., p. 171.

26. Ibid., p. 67.

27. Ibid., pp. 227–229.

28. Chang (1997).

29. Ibid., p. 48.

30. Ibid., p. 119.

31. Benedict (1934). Benedict's use of Apollonian and Dionysian was based on Nietzsche's studies of Greek tragedy.

32. Gorer (1943), Benedict (1946).

33. Benedict (1946), p. 259.

34. Rouhana & Bar-tal (1998), p. 761.

35. *Reducing Youth Gun Violence* (1996), p. 1. The statement is based upon a 1994 policy paper of the Pacific Center for Violence Prevention titled *Preventing Youth Violence: Reducing Access to Firearms.*

36. Zimring & Hawkins (1997).

37. Ibid., pp. 4–5.

38. Ibid., p. 6.

39. Ibid., p. 8.

40. Fingerhut & Kleinman (1990).

41. These reports were taken from the *Washington Post* in a section devoted to the Maryland suburbs. See *Montgomery Weekly*, August 7, 1997.

42. The survey was reported by the American School Health Association in 1989.

43. Fingerhut & Kleinman (1990). The statistics cited were reported by The Centers for Disease Control.

44. Osofsky (1995), p. 783.

45. Ibid.

46. Ibid.

47. Farrell & Bruce (1997).

48. Ibid. These statistics are presented in Figure 2, p. 7.

49. Wandersman & Nation (1998), p. 648.

50. Ibid.

51. Ibid.

52. Students' Reports of School Crime: 1989 and 1995 (1998).

53. Block & Block (1993).

54. Ibid., p. 8.

55. The survey conducted by Louis Harris was cited in *Reducing Youth Gun Violence* (1996), p. 4.

56. Webster, et al. (1993).

57. *Reducing Youth Gun Violence* (1996), p. 5.

58. These statistics are cited in *Reducing Youth Gun Violence* (1996), p. 3.
59. Twomey (1997).
60. Lorion & Saltzman (1993).
61. See Litz, et al. (1997a) and Litz, et al. (1997b).
62. Fitzpatrick & Boldizar (1993).
63. Freeman, et al. (1996).
64. Gil (1996).
65. Tagaki & Platt (1978).
66. Jencks (1992), p. 113.
67. Guerra, et al. (1995), p. 519.
68. Ibid., pp. 525–527.
69. Wandersman & Nation (1998).
70. Kellerman (1993).
71. Courtwright (1998).
72. Ibid., p. 10.
73. Study: Violence Hits 10% of Public Schools (1998).

Chapter 4

1. Garbarino (1995).
2. Huesmann & Guerra (1997).
3. El-Sheikh, et al. (1994).
4. Grych & Fincham (1990), p. 274.
5. Lyons-Ruth (1996), p. 64.
6. Haapasalo & Tremblay (1994).
7. Herrenkohl, et al. (1997), p. 427.
8. Churchill (1958).
9. These findings were reported in a series of studies carried out by D.O. Lewis and his colleagues. See for example Lewis, et al. (1979).
10. Reuterman & Burcky (1989).
11. McCord (1983).
12. Garbarino (1995), pp. 67–68.
13. Bousha & Twentyman (1984).
14. Ibid., p. 113.
15. See the discussion in Loeber & Hay on family structure, p. 396.
16. Kupersmidt, et al. (1995).
17. Shaw, et al. (1994).
18. Ibid. See Table 3, p. 360.
19. Nasby, et al. (1980), p. 461.
20. Ibid., p. 464.
21. Dodge, et al. (1990).
22. Dodge & Newman (1981).
23. Ibid., p. 376.

24. Eckhardt, et al. (1998).

25. See for example students' grasp of English recalled at slaying trial (May 21, 1993). Another tragic story was reported in Arizona where a small child hid herself behind the door of the house intending to surprise her father. She yelled "boo!" when he entered and he responded by firing his pistol, killing her. He thought he was in danger. See Coudroglou (1996).

26. Halperin, et al. (1995).

27. Ollendick (1996), p. 492.

28. Coie, et al. (1992), p. 789.

29. Moskowitz, et al. (1985).

30. Brook, et al. (1992).

31. Stattin & Magnusson (1989).

32. Loeber & Dishion (1983), p. 81.

33. O'Donnell, et al. (1995), p. 529.

34. Stattin & Magnusson (1989), p. 716.

35. O'Donnell, et al. (1995), p. 535.

36. Hinshaw (1992).

37. Huesmann, et al. (1987), p. 236.

38. See widespread use of child soldiers. The internet story was based on a March 1996 article in *The Nation of Bangkok*, written by *Images Asia*.

39. Sly *(*1995). Sly, a staff writer for the *Chicago Tribune*, published her article in the *Tribune* on June 11, 1995. Our citation was the web posting on November 10, 1996.

40. See Israel/Occupied Territories: Children Trained to Become Martyrs. This internet story draws on an article by J.M. Bourget published in *Paris Match*.

41. Moorehead (1995).

42. Chang (1997).

43. Wessells (1997).

44. See Girl Soldiers More Fanatic. This internet story draws on an article by Martin Adler published in *Amnesty Press*, Nov. 4, 1996.

45. Priest (1997).

46. Gibson & Haritos-Fatouros (1986).

47. Rothbaum & Weisz (1994).

48. Bonta (1997), p. 301.

49. For a presentation of Adler's ideas see Ansbacher & Ansbacher (1956).

50. Bonta (1997).

Chapter 5

1. Novaco (1994), p. 321.

2. Alexander (1950).

3. Robbins (1969).

4. Allerhand, et al. (1950), p. 387.
5. Robbins, et al. (1974).
6. Robbins & Tanck (1982).
7. Robbins, et al. (1974), p. 583.
8. Friedman & Rosenman (1974).
9. Booth-Kewley & Friedman (1987), p. 343.
10. Friedman & Ulmer (1984), p. 5.
11. Ibid., p. 31.
12. Ibid., p. 32.
13. Ibid., p. 34.
14. Booth-Kewley & Friedman (1987), pp. 357–358.
15. Ibid., p. 358.
16. Miller, et al. (1996), p. 340.
17. Lyness (1993).
18. Friedman & Ulmer (1984), p. 34.
19. Elander, et al. (1993). See p. 289 for a summary of research findings.
20. McGuire (1972).
21. Haviland & Wiseman (1974).
22. Freud (1959).
23. Robbins & Tanck (1997).
24. Novaco (1994), p. 320.
25. Wells (1931).
26. Novaco (1994), p. 320.
27. Baumeister, et al. (1990).
28. *Violence Between Intimates* (1994), p. 2.
29. Ibid., p. 1.
30. These incidents are described on pp. 37, 34, 22, 36, 28 and 30.
31. *Violence Between Intimates* (1944), p. 1.
32. Ibid., p. 2.
33. Ibid., p. 2.

Chapter 6

1. The shootings in Arkansas and Oregon were widely covered in the newspapers and on television. For an article discussing these events, see Sleek (1998). The subsequent shootings in Colorado were also widely covered.
2. Freedman (1984).
3. Ibid. The research review cited was the work of F.S. Andison.
4. See The Surgeon General's Scientific Advisory Committee on Television and Social Behavior 1972 report *Television and Growing Up: The Impact of Televised Violence.*
5. For a description of the study, see Murray (1988). The study was carried out at several sites; the Universities of California at Santa Barbara, Texas at Austin, North Carolina and Wisconsin.

6. See for example Gerbner (1990).

7. The study is cited in Stossel (1998), p. 82.

8. Huston, et al. (1992), pp. 12–13. See Figures 1.1 and 1.2.

9. Ibid., pp. 53–54.

10. Freedman (1984), p. 228.

11. Wood, et al. (1991), p. 378.

12. Eron, et al. (1972).

13. See the reports of Drabman & Thomas (1974) and Molitor & Hirsch (1994).

14. The incident was cited in Stossel (1998), p. 78.

15. El-Sheikh, et al. (1994).

16. The Tacitus Citation was taken from Bok (1998), p. 18.

17. Ibid., pp. 18–19.

18. All three studies described here were reported in Bushman (1995).

19. Ibid., p. 952.

20. Ibid.

21. Levine (1996). See for example p. 142.

22. Feshbach (1972).

23. Murray (1998).

24. Rosekrans (1967).

25. Murray (1998).

26. See Hattemer & Showers (1995), p. 153.

27. See Commission finds industry video programming rating system acceptable: Adopts technical requirements to enable blocking of video programming (the "v-chip"), (1998).

28. See Separate Statement of Commissioner Gloria Tristani (1998).

Chapter 7

1. Shakespeare (1938), p. 746.

2. Mather's statement was cited in Critchlow (1986), p. 752.

3. Rorabaugh (1979), p. 12.

4. Critchlow, p. 752.

5. Chipman's 1845 statement was cited in Critchlow (1986), p. 754.

6. Isaacs (1977).

7. Isaacs (1979).

8. Steele (1986).

9. Pernanen (1991), pp. 200–201. See in particular Table 9.2, p. 201.

10. Hamberger & Hastings (1988).

11. Saunders (1992).

12. MacDonald (1961). MacDonald reviewed ten studies and found a median value of 54 percent.

13. *Making the Link* (1995).

14. Ibid.

15. Seto & Barbaree (1995).

16. *Making the Link* (1995).

17. Pernanen (1991), pp. 26–27.

18. Boyatzis (1974).

19. Bushman & Cooper (1990), p. 348.

20. Ibid., p. 348.

21. Ibid., p. 342.

22. Steele & Josephs (1990).

23. For reviews of the problem see Hull & Bond (1986) and Bushman & Cooper (1990).

24. Kilpatrick, et al. (1997).

25. Miller, et al. (1987).

26. Magdol, et al. (1997).

Chapter 8

1. Gilje (1996), p. 72.

2. The lines are from Lazarus' poem *The New Colossus* (1883).

3. The description of the events preceding the Haymarket tragedy is based on Avrich's account (1984). See in particular pages 184–193. The description of the Haymarket incident itself is also based on Avrich's book.

4. Ibid., p. 190. Spies' "revenge circular" is in the collection of the Chicago Historical Society.

5. Ibid., p. 193.

6. Ibid., p. 206.

7. Ibid., p. 207.

8. Duberman (1993). The description of the Stonewall riot is based on Duberman's book.

9. This statistic was taken from staff of the *Los Angeles Times'* Understanding the Riots (1992).

10. Ibid., p. 10.

11. Ibid., p. 33.

12. Ibid., p. 59.

13. Ibid., p. 101.

14. Ibid., p. 130.

15. Gilje (1996), see pp. 127–128.

16. Grant (1951). Personal communication. Stories about the Cicero incident appeared in the *New York Times*. For example (June 27, 1951) Negro exclusive banned. Cicero, Ill. is restrained from barring apartment to family, p. 31.

17. Rioting Goes on, Despite Killings (September 24, 1906), *New York Times*.

18. Ibid.

19. Ibid.

20. Ibid.

21. This story is reported in the Special Master's Final Report (March 24, 1994).

22. Smith (1998), p. 750.

Chapter 9

1. Kernis, et al. (1989). When self-esteem becomes inflated, approaching the state of Narcissism, it is likely to lower the threshold for aggressive responding. People who entertain grandiose self-images are likely to react strongly to perceived insults and negative evaluations. See Bushman & Baumeister (1998).

2. Manson & Gilliard (1998).

3. Sullivan (1997).

4. Ibid.

5. Ibid.

6. *Reducing Youth Gun Violence* (1996). These programs are described on p. 15.

7. Ibid., p. 14.

8. Ibid., p. 14.

9. Hausman, et al. (1995).

10. Hausman, et al. (1996).

11. DeJong (undated).

12. Ibid., pp. 11–12.

13. Kingsley, et al. (1997), p. 25.

14. Ibid., p. 19.

15. Ibid., pp. 17–18.

16. Ibid., p. 18.

17. Murray (1998).

18. Lochman, et al. (1995), p. 549.

19. Ibid., p. 557.

20. Ibid.

21. Loeber & Hay (1997). See p. 388.

22. For a discussion of some of these studies, see Prinz, et al. (1994).

23. Ibid.

24. Hammond & Yung (1991).

25. Tate, et al. (1995).

26. Goldstein, et al. (1986) and Goldstein, et al. (1994).

27. Guerra & Slaby (1990).

28. See for example Henggeler, et al. (1992) and Henggeler, et al. (1993).

29. Henggeler, et al. (1992).

Chapter 10

1. Bach (1976).
2. Orwell (1949).
3. For an evaluation of procedures used to treat anger-related problems, see Edmonson & Conger (1996).
4. For a general reference on cognitive therapy, see Beck (1976).
5. Miller & Eisenberg (1988).
6. See, for example, Kanner, et al. (1981).
7. For a discussion of the relation between perfectionism and depression, see Blatt (1995).
8. There is considerable research pointing to the negative effects of rumination on depressed mood. See Rusting & Nolen-Hoeksema (1998), p. 1.
9. Rusting & Nolen-Hoeksema (1998).

Bibliography

Alberts, D. (1994). *Talking About Mime: An Illustrated Guide.* Portsmouth, NH: Heinemann.

Alcohol, Violence, and Aggression (October, 1997). *Alcohol Alert*, No. 38. Rockville, MD: National Institute on Alcohol Abuse and Alcoholism.

Alexander, F. (1950). *Psychosomatic Medicine.* New York: Norton.

Allerhand, M.E., Gough, H.G. & Grais, M.L. (1950). Personality Factors in Neurodermatitis: A Preliminary Study. *Psychosomatic Medicine*, 12, 386–390.

American School Health Association (1989). *The National Adolescent Health Survey: A Report on the Health of America's Youth.* Oakland, CA.

Anderson, C.A. (1989). Temperature and Aggression: Ubiquitous Effects of Heat on Occurrence of Human Violence. *Psychological Bulletin*, 106, 74–96.

Anderson, C.A. & Bushman, B. (February 1998). Will Global Warming Inflame our Tempers? *American Psychological Association Monitor*, 8.

Andison, F.S. (1977). TV Violence and Viewer Aggression: A Cumulation of Study Results, 1956–1976. *Public Opinion Quarterly*, 41, 314–331.

Ansbacher, H.L. & Ansbacher, R.R. (Eds.) (1956). *The Individual Psychology of Alfred Adler.* New York: Basic Books.

Aristotle (1913). Physiognomonica. In W.D. Ross (Ed.) *The Works of Aristotle* (pp. 805–813). Oxford, England: Clarendon.

Averill, J.R. (1983). Studies on Anger and Aggression: Implication for Theories of Emotion. *American Psychologist*, 38, 1145–1160.

Avrich, P. (1984). *The Haymarket Tragedy.* Princeton, NJ: Princeton University Press.

Bach, G.R. (1976). *The Intimate Enemy: How to Fight Fair in Love and Marriage.* New York: Avon.

Baumeister, R.F., Stillwell, A. & Wotman, S.R. (1990). Victim and Perpetrator

Accounts of Interpersonal Conflict: Autobiographical Narratives About Anger. *Journal of Personality and Social Psychology*, 59, 994–1005.

Beck, A.T. (1976). *Cognitive Therapy and the Emotional Disorders*. New York: International Universities Press.

Benedict, R. (1934). *Patterns of Culture*. Boston, MA: Houghton Mifflin.

Benedict, R. (1946). *The Chrysanthemum and the Sword: Patterns of Japanese Culture*. Houghton Mifflin. Reprinted Meridian, 1974.

Bennett, J.W. (1967). *Hutterian Brethren: The Agricultural Economy and Social Organization of a Communal People*. Stanford, CA: Stanford University Press.

Berkowitz, L. (1983). Aversively Stimulated Aggression: Some Parallels and Differences in Research with Animals and Humans. *American Psychologist*, 38, 1135–1144.

Berkowitz, L. (1989). Frustration-aggression Hypothesis: Examination and Reformulation. *Psychological Bulletin*, 106, 59–73.

Berman, M.E., Tracy, J.I. & Coccaro, E.F. (1997). The Serotonin Hypothesis of Aggression Revisited. *Clinical Psychology Review*, 17, 651–665.

Bettencourt, B.A. & Miller, N. (1996). Gender Differences in Aggression as a Function of Provocation: A Meta-Analysis. *Psychological Bulletin*, 119, 422–447.

Block, C.R. & Block, R. (December 1993). Street Gang Crime in Chicago. *National Institute of Justice: Research in Brief*. Washington, D.C.: U.S. Department of Justice.

Bok, S. (1998). *Mayhem: Violence as Public Entertainment*. Reading, MA: Addison-Wesley.

Bonta, B.D. (1997). Cooperation and Competition in Peaceful Societies. *Psychological Bulletin*, 121, 299–320.

Booth-Kewley, S. & Friedman, H.S. (1987). Psychological Predictors of Heart Disease: A Quantitative Review. *Psychological Bulletin*, 101, 343–362.

Borduin, C.M., Mann, B.J., Cone, L.T., Henggeler, S.W., Fucci, B.R., Blaske, D.M. & Williams, R.A. (1995). Multisystemic Treatment of Serious Juvenile Offenders: Long-term Prevention of Criminality and Violence. *Journal of Consulting and Clinical Psychology*, 63, 569–578.

Borke, H. & Su, S. (1972). Perception of Emotional Responses to Social Interactions by Chinese and American Children. *Journal of Cross-Cultural Psychology*, 3, 309–314.

Boucher, J.D. & Carlson, G.E. (1980). Recognition of Facial Expression in Three Cultures. *Journal of Cross-Cultural Psychology*, 11, 263–280.

Bousha, D.M. & Twentyman, C.T. (1984). Mother-child Interactional Style in Abuse, Neglect, and Control Groups. *Journal of Abnormal Psychology*, 93, 106–114.

Boyatzis, R.E. (1974). The effect of Alcohol Consumption on the Aggressive Behavior of Men. *Quarterly Journal of Studies in Alcohol*, 35, 959–972.

Bredemeier, B.J. & Shields, D.Z. (October, 1985). Values and Violence in Sports Today. *Psychology Today*, 19, 22.

Brook, J.S., Whiteman, M.M. & Finch, S. (1992). Childhood Aggression, Adolescent Delinquency, and Drug Use: A Longitudinal Study. *Journal of Genetic Psychology*, 153, 369–383.

Bushman, B.J. (1995). Moderating Role of Trait Aggressiveness in the Effects of Violent Media on Aggression. *Journal of Personality and Social Psychology*, 69, 950–960.

Bushman, B.J. & Baumeister, R.F. (1998). Threatened Egotism, Narcissism, Self-esteem, and Direct and displaced Aggression: Does Self-love or Self-hate Lead to Violence? *Journal of Personality and Social Psychology*, 75, 219–229.

Bushman, B.J. & Cooper, H.M. (1990). Effects of Alcohol on Human Aggression: An Integrative Research Review. *Psychological Bulletin*, 107, 341–354.

Buss, A.H. (1961). *The Psychology of Aggression*. New York: Wiley.

Buss, A.H. & Durkee, A. (1957). An Inventory for Assessing Different Kinds of Hostility. *Journal of Consulting Psychology*, 21, 343–349.

Buss, A.H. & Perry, M. (1992). The Aggression Questionnaire. *Journal of Personality and Social Psychology*, 63, 452–459.

Buss, D.M. & Shackelford, T.K. (1997). Human Aggression in Evolutionary Psychological Perspective. *Clinical Psychology Review*, 17, 605–619.

Calvert, S.L. & Tan, S. (1994). Impact of Virtual Reality on Young Adults' Physiological Arousal and Aggressive Thoughts: Interaction Versus Observation. *Journal of Applied Developmental Psychology*, 15, 125–139.

Chagnon, N.A. (1983). *Yąnomamö: The Fierce People* (Third Edition). New York: Holt, Rinehart and Winston.

Chang, I. (1997). *The Rape of Nanking: The Forgotten Holocaust of World War II*. New York: Basic Books.

Chipman, S. (1845). The Temperance Lecturer; Being Facts Gathered From a Personal Examination of all the Jails and Poor-houses … Showing the Effects of Intoxicating Drinks in Producing Taxes, Pauperism and Crime. Albany, NY.

Churchill, W.S. (1958). *My Early Life: A Roving Commission*. New York: Scribner.

Cloninger, C.R., Sigvardsson, S., Bohman, M. & von Knorring, A.L. (1982). Predisposition to Petty Criminality in Swedish Adoptees, II. Cross-fostering Analysis of Gene-environment Interaction. *Archives of General Psychiatry*, 39, 1242–1249.

Coccaro, E.F. & Kavoussi, R.J. (1997). Fluoxetine and Impulsive Aggressive Behavior in Personality-disorded Subjects. *Archives of General Psychiatry*, 54, 1081–1088.

Coie, J.D., Lockman, J.E., Terry, R. & Hyman, C. (1992). Predicting Early Adolescent Disorder From Childhood Aggression and Peer Rejection. *Journal of Consulting and Clinical Psychology*, 60, 783–792.

Cornell, D.G., Warren, J., Hawk, G., Stafford, E., Oram, G. & Pine, D.

(1996). Psychopathy in Instrumental and Reactive Violent Offenders. *Journal of Consulting and Clinical Psychology.* 64, 783–790.

Commission Finds Industry Video Programming Rating System Acceptable: Adopts Technical Requirements to Enable Blocking of Video Programming (The "V-Chip"). Report No. GN 98-3. (March 12, 1998). *FCC News.*

Coudroglou, A. (1996). Violence as a Social Mutation. *American Journal of Orthopsychiatry,* 66, 323–328.

Courtwright, D.T. (1998). Violence in America. In F. McGuckin (Ed.). *Violence in American Society* (pp. 3–15). New York: Wilson.

Crick, N. & Bigbee, M.A. (1998). Relational and Overt Forms of Peer Victimization: A Multi-informant Approach. *Journal of Consulting and Clinical Psychology,* 66, 337–347.

Crime Watch. (August 7, 1997). The *Washington Post,* MD5.

Critchlow, B. (1986). The Powers of John Barleycorn: Beliefs About the Effects of Alcohol on Social Behavior. *American Psychologist,* 41, 751–764.

Dabbs, J.M., Jr. & Morris, R. (1990). Testosterone, Social Class, and Antisocial Behavior in a Sample of 4,462 Men. *Psychological Science,* 1, 209–211.

DeJong, W. (Undated). Building the Peace: The Resolving Conflict Creatively Program (RCCP). Washington, D.C. National Institute of Justice NCJ 149549.

DiLalla, L.F. & Gottesman I.I. (1991). Biological and Genetic Contributors to Violence—Windom's Untold Tale. *Psychological Bulletin,* 109, 125–129.

Dodge, K.A. & Newman, J.P. (1981). Biased Decision-making Processes in Aggressive Boys. *Journal of Abnormal Psychology,* 90, 375–379.

Dodge, K.A., Price, J.M., Bachorowski, J. & Newman, J.P. (1990). Hostile Attributional Biases in Severely Aggressive Adolescents. *Journal of Abnormal Psychology,* 99, 385–392.

Dollard, J., Doob, L., Miller, N., Mowrer, O. & Sears, R. (1939). *Frustration and Aggression.* New Haven, CT: Yale University Press.

Drabman, R.S. & Thomas, M.H. (1974). Does Media Violence Increase Children's Toleration of Real-life Aggression? *Developmental Psychology,* 10, 418–421.

Drabman, R.S. & Thomas, M.H. (1974). Exposure to Filmed Violence and Children's Toleration of Real-life Aggression. *Personality and Social Psychology Bulletin,* 1, 198–199.

Duberman, J.B. (1993). *Stonewall.* New York: Dutton.

Eckhardt, C.I., Barbour, K.A. & Davison, G.C. (1998). Articulated Thoughts of Maritally Violent and Nonviolent Men During Anger Arousal. *Journal of Consulting and Clinical Psychology,* 66, 259–269.

Eckhardt, C.I. & Kassinove, H. (August 12, 1994). Attitudes Toward Aggressive Behavior, Anger, Expression, and Self-reported Aggression. Paper presented at annual convention of the American Psychological Association, Los Angeles, CA.

Edmonson, C.B. & Conger, J.C. (1996). A Review of Treatment Efficacy for Individuals with Anger Problems: Conceptual Assessment and Methodological Issues. *Clinical Psychology Review*, 16, 251–275.

Ekman, P. (1993). Facial Expression and Emotion. *American Psychologist*, 48, 384–392.

Ekman, P. (1994). Strong Evidence for Universals in Facial Expressions: A Reply to Russell's Mistaken Critique. *Psychological Bulletin*, 115, 268–287.

Elander, J., West, R. & French, D. (1993). Behavioral Correlates of Individual Differences in Road-Traffic Crash Risk: An Examination of Methods and Findings. *Psychological Bulletin*, 113, 279–294.

El-Sheikh, M., Ballard, M. & Cummings, E.M. (1994). Individual Differences in Preschoolers' Physiological and Verbal Responses to Videotaped Angry Interactions. *Journal of Abnormal Child Psychology*, 22, 303–320.

Endicott, K. (1988). Property, Power and Conflict Among the Batek of Malaysia. In T. Ingold, D. Riches & J. Woodburn (Eds.) *Hunters and Gatherers. 2: Property, Power and Ideology* (pp. 110–127). Oxford, England: Berg.

Eron, L.D., Huesmann, L.R., Lefkowitz, M.M. & Walder, L.O. (1972). Does Television Violence Cause Aggression? *American Psychologist*, 27, 253–263.

Farrell, A.D. & Bruce, S.E. (1997). Impact of Exposure to Community Violence on Violent Behavior and Emotional Distress Among Urban Adolescents. *Journal of Clinical Child Psychology*, 26, 2–14.

Fehr, B. & Russell, J.A. (1991). The Concept of Love Viewed from a Prototype Perspective. *Journal of Personality and Social Psychology*, 60, 425–438.

Feinstein, J. (1996). *A Civil War: Army vs. Navy: A Year Inside College Football's Purest Rivalry*. Boston, MA: Little, Brown.

Feshbach, S. (1972). Reality and Fantasy in Filmed Violence. In J. Murray, E. Rubinstein & G. Comstock, (Eds.) *Television and Social Behavior* (pp. 318–345). Washington, D.C.: Dept. H.E.W.

Fingerhut, I.A. & Kleinman, J.C. (1990). International and Interstate Comparisons of Homicide Among Young Males. *Journal of the American Medical Association*, 263, 3292–3295.

Fitness, J. & Fletcher, G.J.O. (1993). Love, Hate, Anger, and Jealousy in Close Relationships: A Prototype and Cognitive Appraisal Analysis. *Journal of Personality and Social Psychology*, 65, 942–958.

Fitzpatrick, K.M. (1993). Exposure to Violence and Presence of Depression Among Low-income African-American Youth. *Journal of Consulting and Clinical Psychology*, 61, 528–531.

Fitzpatrick, K.M. & Boldizar, J.P. (1993). The Prevalence and Consequences of Exposure to Violence Among African-American Youth. *Journal*

American Academy of Child and Adolescent Psychiatry, 32, 424–430.

Freedman, J.L. (1984). Effect of Television Violence on Aggressiveness. *Psychological Bulletin*, 96, 227–246.

Freeman, L.N., Shaffer, D. & Smith, H. (1996). Neglected Victims of Homicide: The Needs of Young Siblings of Murder Victims. *American Journal of Orthopsychiatry*, 66, 337–345.

Freud, S. (1959). *Mourning and Melancholia*. In *Collected Papers*, Vol. 4, 152–170. New York: Basic Books.

Friedman, M. & Rosenman, R. (1974). *Type A Behavior and Your Heart*, New York: Knopf.

Friedman, M. & Ulmer, D. (1984). *Treating Type A Behavior and Your Heart*, New York: Knopf.

Garbarino, J. (1995). *Raising Children in a Socially Toxic Environment*. San Francisco: Jossey-Bass.

Gerbner, G. & Signorielli, N. (1990). *Violence Profile, 1967 Through 1988-89: Enduring Patterns*. Unpublished manuscript, University of Pennsylvania, Annenberg School of Communications Cited in Huston, et al., p. 54.

Gibson, J.T. & Haritos-Fatouros, M. (November 1986). The Education of a Torturer. *Psychology Today*, 20, 50.

Gil, D.G. (1996). Preventing Violence in a Structurally Violent Society: Mission Impossible. *American Journal of Orthopsychiatry*, 66, 77–84.

Gilje, P.A. (1996). *Rioting in America*, Bloomington, Indiana: Indiana University Press.

Girl Soldiers More Fanatic. http://www.rb.se:80/chilwar/chilwar9.htm

Gladue, B.A. (1991). Aggressive Behavioral Characteristics, Hormones, and Sexual Orientation in Men and Women. *Aggressive Behavior*, 17, 313–326.

Gladue, B.A., Boechier, M. & McCaul, K.D. (1989). Hormonal Response to Competition in Human Males. *Aggressive Behavior*, 15, 409–422.

Goldstein, A.P., Glick, B., Reiner, S., Zimmerman, D. & Coultry, T. (1986). *Aggression Replacement Training*. Champaign, IL: Research Press.

Goldstein, A.P. & Glick, B. (1994). Aggression Replacement Training: Curriculum and Evaluation. *Simulation and Gaming*, 25, 9–26.

Gorer, Geoffrey (1943). Themes in Japanese Culture. *Transactions of the New York Academy of Science*, 5, 106–124.

Graham, S. & Hoehn, S. (1995). Children's Understanding of Aggression and Withdrawal as Social Stigmas: An Attributional Analysis. *Child Development*, 66, 1143–1161.

Grant, W.A. (1951). The Circero Place Riots and the Newspapers. Unpublished Report.

Grych, J.H. & Fincham, F.D. (1990). Marital Conflict and Children's Adjustment: A Cognitive-contextual Framework. *Psychological Bulletin*, 108, 267–290.

Guerra, N.G. & Slaby, R.G. (1990). Cognitive Mediators of Aggression in

Adolescent Offenders: 2. Intervention. *Developmental Psychology*, 26, 269–277.

Guerra, N.G., Huesmann, L.R., Tolan, P.H., van Acker, R. & Eron, L.D. (1995). Stressful Events and Individual Beliefs as Correlates of Economic Disadvantage and Aggression Among Urban Children. *Journal of Consulting and Clinical Psychology*, 63, 518–528.

Haapasalo, J. & Tremblay, R.E. (1994). Physically Aggressive Boys from Ages 6 to 12: Family Background, Parenting Behavior, and Prediction of Delinquency. *Journal of Consulting and Clinical Psychology*, 62, 1044–1052.

Halperin, J.M., Newcorn J.H., Matier, K., Bedi, G., Hall, S. & Vanshdeep, S. (1995). Impulsivity and the Initiation of Fights in Children with Disruptive Behavior Disorders. *Journal of Child Psychology and Psychiatry and Allied Disciplines*, 36, 1199–1211.

Hamberger, L.K. & Hastings, J. (1988). Characteristics of Male Spouse Abusers Consistent with Personality Disorders. *Hospital and Community Psychiatry*, 39, 763–770.

Hammond, R.W. & Yung, B.R. (1991). Preventing Violence in At-risk African-American Youth. *Journal of Health Care for the Poor and Underserved*, 2, 359–373.

Harris, J.A., Rushton, J.P., Hampson, E. & Jackson, D.N. (1996). Salivary Testosterone and Self-report Aggressive and Pro-social Personality Characteristics in Men and Women. *Aggressive Behavior*, 22, 321–331.

Hattemer, B. & Showers, R. (1995). Heavy Metal Rock and Gangsta Rap Music Promote Violence, in *Violence in the Media* (Ed. C. Wekesser). San Diego: Greenhaven.

Hausman, A., Pierce, G. & Briggs, L. (1996). Evaluation of a Comprehensive Violence Prevention Education: Effects on Student Behavior. *Journal of Adolescent Health*, 19, 104–110.

Hausman, A.J., Spivak, H. & Prothrow-Stith, D. (1995). Evaluation of a Community-based Youth Violence Prevention Project. *Journal of Adolescent Health*, 17, 353–359.

Haviland, C.V. & Wiseman, H.A.B. (1974). Criminals Who Drive. In *Proceedings of the 18th Annual Convention of the American Association for Automotive Medicine* (pp. 432–439). Toronto, Canada.

Hay, D.F. (1984). Social Conflict in Early Childhood. *Annuals of Child Development*, 1, 1–44.

Hazaleus, S.L. & Deffenbacher, J.L. (1986). Relaxation and Cognitive Treatment of Anger. *Journal of Consulting and Clinical Psychology*, 54, 222–226.

Henggeler, S.W., Melton, G.B., & Smith, L.A. (1992). Family Preservation Using Multisystemic Therapy: An Effective Alternative to Incarcerating Serious Juvenile Offenders. *Journal of Consulting and Clinical Psychology*, 60, 953–961.

Henggeler, S.W., Melton, G.B., Smith, L.A., Schoenwald, S.K. & Hanley, J.H. (1993). Family Preservation Using Multisystemic Treatment: Long-term Follow-up to a Clinical Trial with Serious Juvenile Offenders. *Journal of Child and Family Studies*, 2, 283–293.

Herodotus (1942). *The Persian Wars*. New York: Modern Library.

Herrenkohl, R.C., Egolf, B.P. & Herrenkohl, E.C. (1997). Preschool Antecedents of Adolescent Assaultive Behavior: A Longitudinal Study. *American Journal of Orthopsychiatry*, 67, 422–432.

Hinshaw, S.P. (1992). Externalizing Behavior Problems and Academic Underachievement in Childhood and Adolescence: Causal Relationships and Underlying Mechanisms. *Psychological Bulletin*, III, 127–155.

Hixson, R. (March 24, 1994). Special Master's Final Report. http://www.freenet.scri.fsu.edu/doc/rosewood2.txt

Hochschild, A. (1998). *King Leopold's Ghost: A Story of Greed, Terror and Heroism in Colonial Africa*. New York: Houghton Mifflin.

Huesmann, L.R., Eron, L.D. & Yarmel, P.W. (1987). Intellectual Functioning and Aggression. *Journal of Personality and Social Psychology*, 52, 232–240.

Huesmann, L.R., Guerra, N.G. (1997). Children's Normative Beliefs About Aggression and Aggressive Behavior. *Journal of Personality and Social Psychology*, 72, 408–419.

Hull, J.G. & Bond, C.F., Jr. (1986). Social and Behavioral Consequences of Alcohol Consumption and Expectancy: A Meta-Analysis. *Psychological Bulletin*, 99, 347–360.

Huston, A.C., Donnerstein, E., Fairchild, H., Feshbach, N.D., Katz, P.A., Murray, J.P., Rubinstein, E.A., Wilcox, B.L. & Zuckerman, D. (1992). *Big World, Small Screen: The Role of Television in American Society*. Lincoln, Nebraska: University of Nebraska Press.

Isaacs, M. (1977). Stereotyping by Children of the Effects of Drinking on Adults. *Journal of Studies on Alcohol*, 38, 913–921.

Isaacs, M. (1979). College Students' Expectations of the Results of Drinking. *Journal of Studies on Alcohol*, 40, 476–479.

Israel/Occupied Territories: Children Trained to Become Martyrs. http://www.rb.se:80/chilwar/chilwar9.htm

Ito, T.A., Miller, N. & Pollock, V.E. (1996). Alcohol and Aggression: A Meta-analysis of the Moderating Effects of Inhibition Cues, Triggering Events, and Self-focused Attention. *Psychological Bulletin*, 120, 60–82.

Izard, C.E. (1980). Cross-cultural Perspectives on Emotion and Emotion Communication. In H. Triandis & W. Lonner (Eds.). *Handbook of Cross-cultural Psychology: Basic Processes* (Vol 3, pp. 185–222). Boston: Allyn & Bacon.

Jencks, C. (1992). *Rethinking Social Policy*, Cambridge, MA: Harvard University Press.

Kanner, A.D., Coyne, J.C., Schaefer, C. & Lazarus, R.S. (1981). Comparison of Two Modes of Stress Measurement: Daily Hassles and Uplifts Versus Major Life Events. *Journal of Behavioral Medicine*, 4, 1–39.

Kellerman, A. (1993). Gun Ownership as a Risk Factor for Homicide in the Home. *New England Journal of Medicine*, 329.

Kernis, M.H., Grannemann, B.D. & Barclay, L.C. (1989). Stability and Level of Self-esteem as Predictors of Anger Arousal and Hostility. *Journal of Personality and Social Psychology*, 56, 1013–1022.

Kiester, E. Jr. (July, 1984). The Uses of Anger. *Psychology Today*, 18, 26.

Kilpatrick, D.G., Acierno, R., Resnick, H.S., Saunders, B.E. & Best, C.L. (1997). A 2-year Longitudinal Analysis of the Relationships Between Violent Assault and Substance Abuse in Women. *Journal of Consulting and Clinical Psychology*, 65, 834–847.

Kingsley, C.T., McNeely, J.B. & Gibson, J.O. (1997). *Community Building Coming of Age*, Washington, D.C.: Urban Institute.

Kraybill, D.B. (1989). *The Riddle of Amish Culture*. Baltimore, MD: Johns Hopkins University Press.

Kupersmidt, J.B., Griesler, P.C., DeRosier, M.E., Patterson, C.J., Davis, P.W. (1995). Childhood Aggression and Peer Relations in the Context of Family and Neighborhood Factors. *Child Development*, 66, 360–375.

Leary, T. (1957). *Interpersonal Diagnosis of Personality*. New York: Roland Press.

Levine, M. (1996). Viewing Violence: How Media Violence Affects Your Child's and Adolescent's Development. New York: Doubleday.

Levy, R.I. (1973). *Tahitians: Mind and Experience in the Society Islands*. Chicago: University of Chicago Press.

Lewis, D.O., Shanok, S.S. & Balla, D.A. (1979). Perinatal Difficulties, Head and Face Trauma, and Child Abuse in the Medical Histories of Seriously Delinquent Children. *American Journal of Psychiatry*, 136, 419–423.

Litz, B.T., King, L.A., King, D.W., Orsillo, S.M. & Friedman, M.J. (1997b). Warriors as Peacekeepers: Features of the Somalia Experience and PTSD. *Journal of Consulting and Clinical Psychology*, 65, 1001–1010.

Litz, B.T., Orsillo, S.M., Friedman, M., Ehlich, P. & Batres, A. (1997a). An Investigation of the Psychological Sequelae Associated with Peacekeeping Duty in Somalia for United States Military Personnel. *American Journal of Psychiatry*, 154, 178–184.

Lochman, J.E. & the Conduct Problems Prevention Research Group (1995). Screening of Child Behavior Problems for Prevention Programs at School Entry. *Journal of Consulting and Clinical Psychology*, 63, 549–559.

Loeber, R. & Dishion, T. (1983). Early Predictors of Male Delinquency: A Review. *Psychological Bulletin*, 94, 68–99.

Loeber, R. & Hay, D. (1997). Key Issues in the Development of Aggression and Violence from Children to Early Adulthood. *Annual Review of Psychology*, 48, 371–410.

Lorion, R.L. & Saltzman, W. (1993). Children's Exposure to Community Violence: Following a Path from Concern to Research to Action. *Psychiatry*, 56, 55–65.

Lyness, S.A. (1993). Predictors of Differences Between Type A and B

Individuals in Heart Rate and Blood Pressure Reactivity. *Psychological Bulletin*, 114, 266–295.

Lyons-Ruth K. (1996). Attachment Relationships Among Children with Aggressive Problems: The Role of Disorganized Early Attachment Patterns. *Journal of Consulting and Clinical Psychology*, 64, 64–73.

MacDonald, J.M. (1961): *The Murderer and His Victim*. Springfield, IL: Charles C. Thomas.

Magdol, L., Moffitt, T.E., Caspi, A., Newman, D.L., Fagan, J. & Silva, P.A. (1997). Gender Differences in Partner Violence in a Birth Cohort of 21-Year-Olds: Bridging the Gap Between Clinical and Epidemiological Approaches. *Journal of Consulting and Clinical Psychology*, 65, 68–78.

Making the Link: Domestic Violence and Alcohol and Other Drugs. (Spring 1995). Rockville, MD: Substance Abuse and Mental Health Services Administration.

Malinosky-Rummell, R. & Hansen, D.J. (1993). Long-term Consequences of Childhood Physical Abuse. *Psychological Bulletin*, 114, 68–79.

Manson, D.A. & Gilliard, D.K. (June, 1998). Presale Handgun Checks, 1997. *Bureau of Justice Statistics Bulletin*, NCJ 171130.

Marlatt, G.A. & Rohsenow, D. (1980). Cognitive Processes in Alcohol Use: Expectancy and the Balanced Placebo Design. In N.K. Mello (Ed.). *Advances in Substance Abuse: Behavioral and Biological Research*. Greenwich, CT: JAI Press.

McCord, J. (1983). A Forty Year Perspective on the Effects of Child Abuse and Neglect. *Child Abuse and Neglect*, 7, 265–270.

McGuire, F.L. (1972). A Study of Methodological and Psycho-social Variables in Accident Research. JSAS: Catalogue of Selected Documents in Psychology, 2, 91–92. (Ms. No. 195).

McMahon, R.J. (1994). Diagnosis, Assessment, and Treatment of Externalizing Problems in Children: The Role of Longitudinal Data. *Journal of Consulting and Clinical Psychology*, 62, 901–917.

Mesquita, B. & Frijda, N.H. (1992). Cultural Variations in Emotions: A Review. *Psychological Bulletin*, 112, 179–204.

Mikolic, J.M., Parker, J.C. & Pruitt, D.G. (1997). Escalation in Response to Persistent Annoyance: Groups Versus Individuals and Gender Effects. *Journal of Personality and Social Psychology*, 72, 151–163.

Miles, D.R. & Carey, G. (1997). Genetic and Environmental Architecture of Human Aggression. *Journal of Personality and Social Psychology*, 72, 207–217.

Miller, B.A., Downs, W.R., Gondoli, D.M. & Keil, A. (1987). The Role of Childhood Sexual Abuse in the Development of Alcoholism in Women. *Violence and Victims*, 2, 157–172.

Miller, P.A. & Eisenberg, N. (1988). The Relation of Empathy to Aggressive and Externalizing/Antisocial Behavior. *Psychological Bulletin*, 103, 324–344.

Miller, T.Q., Smith, T.W., Turner, C.W., Guijarro, M.L. & Hullet, A.J.

(1996). A Meta-analytic Review of Research on Hostility and Physical Health. *Psychological Bulletin*, 119, 322–348.

Molitor, F. & Hirsch, K.W. (1994). Children's Toleration of Real-life Aggression After Exposure to Media Violence: A Replication of the Drubman and Thomas Studies. *Child Study Journal*, 24, 191–207.

Moorehead, C. (1995). Sudan's Boy Soldiers. *Index on Censorship*, Issue 1/95. See also http://www.oneworld.org:80/textver/index_oc/samples/hr.html

Moskowitz, D.S., Schwartzman, A.E. & Ledingham, J.E. (1985). Stability and Change in Aggression and Withdrawal in Middle Childhood and Early Adolescence. *Journal of Abnormal Psychology*, 94, 30–41.

Munch, P.A. (1945). *Sociology of Tristan da Cunha*. Oslo, Norway: Det Norske Videnskaps-Akademi.

Murray, B. (June 1988). Study says TV Violence Still Seen as Heroic, Glamorous. *American Psychological Association Monitor*, p.16.

Murray, B. (July 1998). Communities 'Fighting Back' to Quash Neighborhood Crime. *American Psychological Association Monitor*, 35–36.

Nasby, W., Hayden, B. & DePaulo, B.M. (1980). Attributional Bias Among Aggressive Boys to Interpret Unambiguous Social Stimuli as Displays of Hostility. *Journal of Abnormal Psychology*, 89, 459–468.

Norberg-Hodge, H. (1991). *Ancient Futures: Learning From Ladakh*. San Francisco: Sierra Club Books.

Novaco, R.W. (1975). *Anger Control: The Development and Evaluation of an Experimental Treatment*. Lexington, MA: D.C. Heath.

Novaco, R.W. (1994). Clinical Problems of Anger and its Assessment and Regulation Through a Stress Coping Skills Approach. In W. O'Donohue & L. Krasner (Eds.), *Handbook of Psychological Skills Training: Clinical Techniques and Applications*. Allyn & Bacon, pp. 320–338.

Nowlis, V. & Green, R.F. (1958; revised 1963). *Adjective Check List*, Mimeographed.

O'Donnell, J., Hawkins, J.D. & Abbott, R.D. (1995). Predicting Serious Delinquency and Substance Abuse Among Aggressive Boys. *Journal of Consulting and Clinical Psychology*, 63, 529–537.

Ollendick, T.H. (1996). Violence in Youth: Where do we go from Here? Behavior Therapy's Response. *Behavior Therapy*, 27, 485–514.

Olweus, D. (1979). Stability of Aggressive Reaction Patterns in Males: A Review. *Psychological Bulletin*, 86, 852–875.

"One Day Second Lieutenant Ono Said to Us" (1982). Quoted in Wilson, Dick *When Tigers Fight: The Story of the Sino-Japanese War 1937–1945*. New York: Viking, p. 80. Cited in Chang, pp. 56–57.

Orwell, G. (1949). *1984*. New York: Harcourt, Brace.

Osofsky, J.D. (1995). The Effects of Exposure to Violence on Young Children. *American Psychologist*, 50, 782–788.

Overing, J. (1986). Images of Cannibalism, Death and Domination in a "Non-Violent" Society. In D. Riches (Ed.), *The Anthropology of Violence* (pp. 86–101). Oxford, England: Blackwell.

Pan, P.P. & Thomas-Lester, A. Bicyclist Guns Down Motorist. The *Washington Post*, October 9, 1997, p. 1.

Pepler, D.J., Craig, W.M. & Roberts, W.L. (1998). Observations of Aggressive and Nonaggressive Children on the School Playground. *Merrill Palmer Quarterly*, 44, 55–76.

Pernanen, K. (1991). *Alcohol in Human Violence*, New York: Guilford.

Peterson, L., Ewigman, B. & Vandivee, T. (1994). Role of Parental Anger in Low-income Women: Discipline Strategy, Perceptions of Behavior Problems, and the Need for Control. *Journal of Clinical Child Psychology*, 23, 435–443.

Priest, D. (March 3, 1997). Engendering a Warrior Spirit: Women Easily Assimilate in U.S. Armed Forces in Bosnia. The *Washington Post*, A-1.

Prinz, R.J., Blechman, E.A. & Dumas, J.E. (1994). An Evaluation of Peer Coping-Skills Training for Childhood Aggression. *Journal of Clinical Child Psychology*, 23, 193–203.

Prothrow-Stith, D. (1987). *Violence Prevention Curriculum for Adolescents*. Newton, MA: Education Development Center.

Reducing Youth Gun Violence: An Overview of Programs and Initiatives (May, 1996). Washington, D.C.: Office of Juvenile Justice and Delinquency Prevention, U.S. Department of Justice.

Reuterman, N.A. & Burcky, W.D. (1989). Dating Violence in High School: A Profile of the Victims. *Psychology: A Journal of Human Behavior*, 26, 1–9.

Rioting Goes On, Despite Troops (Sept. 24, 1906). *New York Times*. Cited Georgia Stories: History Online. http://www.ceismc.gatedi.edu/ga

Robbins, P.R. (1969). Personality and Psychosomatic Illness: A Selective Review of Research. *Genetic Psychology Monographs*, 80, 51–90.

Robbins, P.R., Meyersburg, H.A. & Tanck, R.H. (1974). Interpersonal Stress and Physical Complaints, *Journal of Personality Assessment* 38, 578–585.

Robbins, P.R. & Tanck, R.H. (1978). A Factor Analysis of Coping Behaviors. *Journal of Clinical Psychology*, 34, 379–380.

Robbins, P.R. & Tanck, R.H. (1982). Further Research Using a Psychological Diary Technique to Investigate Psychosomatic Relationships. *Journal of Clinical Psychology*, 38, 356–359.

Robbins, P.R. & Tanck, R.H. (1992). Stress, Coping Techniques, and Depressed Affect: Explorations Within a Normal Sample. *Psychological Reports*, 70, 147–152.

Robbins, P.R. & Tanck, R.H. (1997). Anger and Depressed Affect: Interindividual and Intraindividual Perspectives. *Journal of Psychology*, 131, 489–500.

Rorabaugh, W.J. (1979). *The Alcoholic Republic: An American Tradition*. New York: Oxford University Press.

Rosaldo, M.Z. (1980). *Knowledge and Passion: Llongot Notions of Self and Social Life*. Cambridge, England: Cambridge University Press.

Rosekrans, M.A. (1967). Imitation in Children as a Function of Perceived Similarities to a Social Model of Vicarious Reinforcement. *Journal of Personality and Social Psychology*, 7, 305–317.

Rothbaum, F. & Weisz, J.R. (1994). Parental Caregiving and Child Externalizing Behavior in Nonclinical Samples: A Meta-analysis. *Psychological Bulletin*, 116, 55–74.

Rouhana, N.N. & Bar-tal, D. (1998). Psychological Dynamics of Intractable Ethnonational Conflicts: The Israeli-Palestinian Case. *American Psychologist*, 53, 761–770.

Rubin, J. (1986). The Emotion of Anger: Some Conceptual and Theoretical Issues. *Professional Psychology: Research and Practice*, 17, 115–124.

Russell, J.A. (1994). Is There Universal Recognition of Emotion from Facial Expression? A Review of the Cross-cultural Studies. *Psychological Bulletin*, 115, 102–141.

Russell, J.A. & Fehr, B. (1994). Fuzzy Concepts in a Fuzzy Hierarchy: Varieties of Anger. *Journal of Personality and Social Psychology*, 67, 186–205.

Rusting, C.L. & Nolen-Hoeksema, S. (1998). Regulating Responses to Anger: Effects of Rumination and Distraction on Angry Mood. *Journal of Personality and Social Psychology*, 74, 790–803.

Rys, G.S. & Bear, G.G. (1997). Relational Aggression and Peer Relations: Gender and Developmental Issues. *Merrill-Palmer Quarterly*, 43, 87–106.

Saunders, D.G. (1992). A Typology of Men Who Batter: Three Types Derived from Cluster Analysis. *American Journal of Orthopsychiatry*, 62, 264–275.

Scherer, K.R., Wallbott, H.G., Matsumato, D. & Kudoh, T. (1988). Emotional Experience in Cultural Context: A Comparison Between Europe, Japan, and the United States. In K.R. Scherer (Ed.), *Facets of Emotions* (pp. 5–30). Hillsdale, NJ: Erlbaum.

Schieffelin, E.D. (1983). Anger and Shame in the Tropical Forest: An Affect as a Cultural System in Papua New Guinea. *Ethos*, 11, 181–191.

Schwartz, J. (March 26, 1998). Two Boys Charged with Murder. The *Washington Post*, A-1.

Separate Statement of Commissioner Gloria Tristani (March 12, 1998). In Commission Finds Industry Video Programming Rating System Acceptable. Adopts Technical Requirements to Enable Blocking of Video Programming (The "V-Chip"). *FCC News*.

Seto, M.C. & Barbaree, H.E. (1995). The role of Alcohol in Sexual Aggression. *Clinical Psychology Review*, 15, 545–566.

Shakespeare, W. (1938). *Shakespeare: Twenty-Three Plays and the Sonnets*. T.M. Parott (ed.), New York: Scribners.

Sharkin, B.S. (1988). The Measurement and Treatment of Client Anger in Counseling. *Journal of Counseling and Development*, 66, 361–365.

Shaw, D.S., Keenan, K. & Vondra, J.I. (1994). Developmental Precursors of Externalizing Behavior: Ages 1 to 3. *Developmental Psychology*, 30, 355–364.

Shreeve, J. (1995). *The Neandertal Enigma: Solving the Mystery of Modern Human Origins*, New York: Avon.

Sleek, S. (August 1998). Experts Scrambling on School Shootings. *American Psychological Association Monitor*, p.1.

Sly, L. (June 11, 1995). The Child Soldiers. *Chicago Tribune*. See also http://www.chicago tribune.com:80/news/zaire/child.htm

Smith, D.N. (1998). The Psychoculture Roots of Genocide: Legitimacy and Crisis in Rwanda. *American Psychologist*, 53, 743–753.

Special Master's Final Report (March 24, 1994). Submitted House of Representatives, State of Florida. http://www.freenet.scri.fsu. edu/doc/rose-wood2.txt

Spielberger, C.D., Jacobs, G., Russell, S. & Crane, R. (1983). Assessment of Anger: The State-Trait Anger Scale. In J.N. Butcher & C.D. Spielberger (Eds.), *Advances in Personality Assessment* (Vol. 2, pp. 159–187). Hillsdale, NJ: Lawrence Erlbaum Associates.

Spielberger, C.D. & Sydeman, S.J. (1994). State-Trait Anxiety Inventory and State-Trait Anger Expression Inventory. In M.E. Maruish (Ed.), *The Use of Psychological Tests for Treatment Planning and Outcome Assessment*. Hillsdale, NJ: LEA, pp. 292–321.

Staff, the *Los Angeles Times* (1992). Understanding the Riots: Los Angeles Before and After The Rodney King Case. *Los Angeles Times*.

Stattin, H. & Magnusson, D. (1989). The Role of Early Aggressive Behavior in the Frequency, Seriousness, and Types of Later Crime. *Journal of Consulting and Clinical Psychology*, 57, 710–718.

Steele, C.M. (January 1986). What Happens When you Drink Too Much? *Psychology Today*, 20, 48.

Steele, C.M. & Josephs, R.A. (1990). Alcohol Myopia: Its Prized and Dangerous Effects. *American Psychologist*, 45, 921–933.

Steinbeck, J. (1962). *Travels with Charley: In Search of America*, New York: Viking.

Stossel, S. (1998). The Man Who Counts the Killings. In F. McGuckin (Ed.), *Violence in American Society* (pp. 77–99). New York: Wilson.

Students' Grasp of English Recalled at Slaying Trial. (May 21, 1992). *Washington Post*, p. A-6.

Students' Reports of School Crime: 1989 and 1995 (1998). Washington, D.C.: Bureau of Justice Statistics, NCJ 169607.

Study: Violence Hits 10% of Public Schools (March 20, 1998). *Washington Post*, A3.

Sullivan, K. (November 7, 1997). Turning Against Guns in Wake of Slaughter. The *Washington Post*, A-27.

Surgeon General's Scientific Advisory Committee on Television and Social Behavior (1972). *Television and Growing Up: The Impact of Televised Violence*. Washington, D.C.: U.S. Government Printing Office.

Tagaki, P. & Platt, T. (1978). Behind the Gilded Ghetto: An Analysis of Race, Class and Crime in Chinatown. *Crime and Social Justice, 9,* 2–25.

Tate, D.C., Reppucci, N.D. & Mulvey, E.P. (1995). Violent Juvenile Delinquents: Treatment Effectiveness and Implications for Future Action. *American Psychologist, 50,* 777–781.

Thucydides (1934). *The Complete Writings of Thucydides.* New York: Modern Library.

Trinkaus, E. & Shipman, P. (1994). *The Neandertals: Of Skeletons, Scientists, and Scandal.* New York: Vintage.

Tristani, G. (March 12, 1998). Separate Statement of Commissioner Gloria Tristani. *FCC News.* Washington, D.C.

Tuchman, B.W. (1988). *The First Salute.* New York: Knopf.

Twomey, S. (April 7, 1997). Shades of Slaughter on the Sidewalk. *Washington Post,* B-1.

Van Goozen, S., Cohen-Kettenis, P.T., Gooren, L.J.G., Frijda, N. & Van de Poll, N. (1995). Gender Differences in Behavior: Activating Effects of Cross-sex Hormones. *Psychoneuroendocrinology, 20,* 343–363.

Van Goozen, S., Frijda, N. & Van de Poll, N. (1994). Anger and Aggression in Women: Influence of Sports Choice and Testosterone Administration. *Aggressive Behavior, 20,* 213–222.

Violence Against Women: A Week in the Life of America (October, 1992). Report prepared by the majority staff of the United States Senate Judiciary Committee.

Violence Between Intimates (November 1994). Office of Justice Programs, U.S. Department of Justice NCJ—149259.

Vuchinich, S. (October 1985). Arguments, Family Style. *Psychology Today,* 19, 40.

Wandersman, A. & Nation, M. (1998). Urban Neighborhoods and Mental Health: Psychological Contributions to Understanding Toxicity, Resilience, and Interventions. *American Psychologist, 53,* 647–656.

Webster, D.W., Gainer, P.S. & Champion, H.R. (1993). Weapon Carrying Among Inner-city Junior High School Students: Defensive Behavior vs. Aggressive Delinquency. *American Journal of Public Health, 83,* 11, 1604–1608.

Wells, H.G. (1931). *The Time Machine.* New York: Random House.

Wessells, M. (November-December 1997). Child Soldiers. *Bulletin of the Atomic Scientists,* 32–39.

Whitman, W. (1995). *Specimen Days.* Mineola, NY: Dover Press.

Wickless, C. & Kirsch, I. (1988). Cognitive Correlates of Anger, Anxiety, and Sadness. *Cognitive Therapy and Research, 12,* 369–377.

Wilkes, J. (June 1987). Murder in Mind. *Psychology Today,* 21, 26.

Wilson, J.Q. (1988). Hostility in America. In F. McGuckin (Ed.), *Violence in American Society* (pp. 39–45). New York: Wilson.

Widespread Use of Child Soldiers (1996). http://www.rb.se:80/chilwar/chilwar9.htm

Windom, C.S. (1989). Does Violence Beget Violence? A Critical Examination of the Literature. *Psychological Bulletin*, 106, 3–28.

Wood, W., Wong, F.Y. & Chachere, J.G. (1991). Effects of Media Violence on Viewers' Aggression in Unconstrained Social Interaction. *Psychological Bulletin*, 109, 371–383.

Yukio, O. (1985). Those in the First Row Were Beheaded. Reports and Recollections of Japanese Military Correspondents. Tokyo: Tokuma Shoten, cited in Chang, p. 56.

Zimring, F.E. & Hawkins, G. (1997). *Crime Is Not the Problem: Lethal Violence in America*. New York: Oxford University Press.

Zukerman, M. & Lubin, B. (1965). *Manual for the Multiple Affective Adjective Checklist*. San Diego, CA: Educational and Industrial Testing Service.

Index